PRAISE

EARLY PUBER

D0286583

"Dr. Kaplowitz has produced an excellent resource on recent issues and controversies regarding early puberty in girls. His ability to write about a complicated medical area in terms that families can understand will help many parents and children who have questions about pubertal events and whether or not treatments might be needed under certain circumstances."

—MARCIA E. HERMAN-GIDDENS, PA, DrPH
Senior Fellow, NC Child Advocacy Institute
Adjunct Professor, School of Public Health, UNC-CH

"This is a practical, illuminating, informative book on precocious puberty that provides guidance and well-distilled practical information for parents concerned and confused by having a child who has begun sexual development at an early age. Dr. Kaplowitz, a renowned, experienced, and compassionate pediatric endocrinologist, with a background of vast experience in caring for children with precocious puberty, offers a compelling book that discusses the causes, diagnosis, treatment, and behavioral aspects of precocious puberty."

—MELVIN M. GRUMBACH, M.D.
Edward B. Shaw Professor of Pediatrics
Department of Pediatrics, University of California

Early Puberty in Girls

THE ESSENTIAL GUIDE

TO COPING WITH

THIS COMMON PROBLEM

Paul Kaplowitz, M.D., Ph.D.

BALLANTINE BOOKS NEW YORK

To my wife and best friend, Lisa.

To the families of the girls I have seen for early puberty
from the Richmond, Virginia area who have shared their
stories and concerns with me, helping me learn how
to manage this common but challenging problem.

CONTENTS

PUBERTY IN
THE HEADLINES

O n February 20, 2001, the subject of early puberty and the normally low-profile academic discipline of pediatric endocrinology graced the front page of the *New York Times*. In an article titled "Doubters Fault Theory Finding Earlier Puberty," science writer Gina Kolata brought to national attention what had previously been a minor disagreement among specialists in my field, and I found myself at the center of the controversy.

At issue was a study published in April 1997 that appeared to show that girls, especially black girls, were starting puberty at earlier ages than previous studies had documented.[1] As a member of the Drug and Therapeutics Committee of the Lawson Wilkins Pediatric Endocrine Society (LWPES), I was asked, along with my colleague Dr. Sharon Oberfield, to review the study and report to the membership our opinion of its scientific validity. I reviewed the paper in detail, read the earlier literature on the subject, and interviewed the lead author, Dr. Marcia Herman-Giddens. Dr. Oberfield and I eventually concluded that the study, in which the stage of puberty was determined in over seventeen thousand girls between ages 3 and 12, was not perfect but provided the most reliable and current data yet on the timing of puberty in girls in the United States. We wrote up our findings and recommendations, the most controversial of which was that we acknowledged that girls are maturing earlier than in the past, and that our guidelines on the age at which puberty should be considered "precocious" reflect this change. We suggested revising the definition for when breast or pubic hair development was too early from age 8 to age 7 for white girls and to age 6 for black girls. The paper was reviewed by the members of the Drug and Therapeutics Committee of LWPES in May 1998, and a revised draft then went to the Executive Committee of LWPES; with a few minor changes, it was approved. Although the paper was never put to a vote of the entire LWPES, it did have the approval of the leadership of the society.

The first rumblings of conflict came when we got back the reviews from the first journal to which we submitted our paper. One of the reviewers liked the paper, while the other reviewer argued forcefully that the original study was so flawed that any recommendations based upon it were also flawed. We resubmitted the paper but it was rejected, so we next sent the paper to *Pediatrics*, the official journal of the American Academy of Pediatrics, the largest organization of pediatricians in the country. Two reviewers looked favorably on what we had written, and after more changes (it had probably been through about fifteen drafts by then), it was published in the October 1999 issue of *Pediatrics*.[2]

Within a few weeks, calls from reporters began coming

in, and articles began appearing. On October 26, 1999, San-
dra Boodman of the *Washington Post* headlined her article
"New Guidelines Say Early Puberty May Be Normal."[3] It
started, "Girls as young as 6 or 7 years old who display the
first signs of puberty are in many cases normal and do not
routinely require workups by specialists or injections of
hormones to delay maturation, according to new recommendations by endocrinologists." I pointed out that the new
recommendations in our article reflected a realization that
the standards we had been using for when puberty in girls
should be considered too early are really out of date.

A few days later, on November 1, the *Philadelphia Inquirer* weighed in with its take on the puberty problem with
the headline "Early Maturing in Girls Is Common, Experts
Say."[4] Its author, Marie McCullough, did an excellent job reviewing the topic. She also pointed out a recurring theme in
the debate over early puberty, which is that although breast
development seems to be starting earlier, the average age at
which white girls have their first period has not changed significantly in the past forty or fifty years. A discussion followed on the social implications of early puberty, including
the question of whether schools should start teaching kids
about puberty earlier than the fifth grade.

A month later, on November 30, Jane Brody made early
puberty the subject of her "Personal Health" column titled
"Yesterday's Precocious Puberty Is Norm Today."[5] "Many
parents become worried when their 7- or 8-year-old daughters begin to develop breasts or grow pubic hair." They wonder if the hormonal changes of puberty will adversely affect
their daughters' behavior, moods, or physical growth and if
girls who are still immature can adjust to early physical maturation. She went on to say, "But whatever the reasons, the

phenomenon is real and, to many parents, worrisome. The new report by [Dr.] Kaplowitz . . . [and Dr.] Oberfield . . . should prove reassuring." She went on to give a lucid summary of all the key points made in our article, including the warning signs indicating when puberty in 6-to-8-year-olds might represent a more serious problem requiring evaluation and treatment.

As 1999 turned into 2000, I fully expected that the puberty story would fade from the news, but the calls and e-mails requesting interviews continued. The *Wall Street Journal* ran a story by Tara Parker-Pope in the July 21, 2000, issue titled "Rise in Early Puberty Causes Parents to Ask, 'When Is It Too Soon?' "[6] The mother of an 8-year-old who had early breast development and mood swings was concerned that "she wasn't prepared emotionally to have breasts and for boys to look at her" and said that the girl had started doing better once she began taking shots to suppress her puberty. I countered that a lot of healthy 7-year-olds undergoing early puberty appeared to be handling it very well. By this time I was saying the same things over and over, and I assumed people would soon get tired of the subject. I was wrong.

The October 2000 issue of *Time* put the early-puberty story right on its cover, with a picture of a young girl wearing a bra. The article, titled "Teens Before Their Time,"[7] quoted several parents on their experiences with early-maturing girls, reviewed the Herman-Giddens study, and discussed several of the popular theories as to why this was happening. Although many people were trying to link earlier puberty to hormones and chemicals in the environment, I and several others who were interviewed spoke out in favor of a more pervasive and well-documented problem, the fattening of American children. I argued that we have long known that overweight girls tend to mature earlier than normal-weight or thin girls. I speculated that the link between obesity and earlier puberty could be a protein called leptin, which is produced by fat cells and which seems to be necessary for the progression of puberty (see chapter 5 for a more detailed discussion of this idea). My colleague Dr. Michael Freemark at Duke University pointed out that "overweight girls have more insulin circulating in their blood, and these higher levels of insulin appear to stimulate the production of sex hormones from the ovary and the adrenal glands." The appearance of the early-puberty story on the cover of *Time* apparently got the attention of the producers of NBC's *Today*, who contacted me and two experts on child development to appear with Katie Couric and discuss the "crisis" of early-maturing girls, which aired on the morning of October 25.

A rather different view of the possible cause of early puberty was presented in an article that appeared in the *New York Times Magazine* on December 24, 2000. Lisa Belkin, in an article titled "The Making of an 8-Year-Old Woman,"[8] discussed the possible roles of obesity, chemicals in the environment, and food additives, but she also raised the possibility that social factors could play a role. She quoted a study showing that young girls raised in households without their biological fathers seem to go through puberty somewhat earlier than girls who maintained a close relationship with their fathers. The researcher, Jay Belsky, a developmental psychologist, also reported that "those girls who matured earlier were the same girls who had more distant family relationships."

Up to this point, the media coverage of the story had taken the view that earlier puberty in girls was an established fact, and focused on what it meant for kids and their parents and why it was happening. But beneath the surface, there were signs that a segment of the pediatric endocrine community was ready to mount a challenge. A letter published in *Pediatrics* in September 2000, signed by Dr. Robert Rosenfield of the University of Chicago and seven colleagues, took careful aim at the 1997 study that had started the whole cycle of puberty stories.[9] It argued that the Herman-Giddens study was fatally flawed because the seventeen thousand subjects had not been selected at random, introducing what could have been serious bias into the results. Any girl between the ages of 3 and 12 who was seen between July 1992 and September 1993 in one of sixty-five participating pediatric offices and who was going to have a complete physical exam (usually a well-child exam) was invited to participate. The letter stated, "One can postulate that a number of girls are brought to their pediatrician with the concern about early onset of breast buds or pubic hair as a hidden agenda, not a stated complaint. . . . In support of the possibility that the study may be flawed was the notable finding in the same practices that age of menarche averaged . . . 12.88 years in whites; this is not clearly different from that reported over 25 years ago, at which time menarche occurred at 12.7 ± 1.0 years . . . Furthermore, liberalizing the definition of normal carries the risk of overlooking pathology. Therefore, we are of the opinion that a well-designed study is necessary before a conclusion can be drawn about the normal age of puberty."

Since the letter was so critical of the 1997 study, Dr. Herman-Giddens and two of her coauthors were asked to respond. They suggested that it was unlikely that a large enough percentage of parents to affect the findings would be reluctant to bring up a concern about puberty even though that was the reason for the visit. They also pointed out that earlier onset puberty has been found to be associated with a longer period of time until menses, which could readily explain why breast development could be starting earlier with little change in the average age of menarche.

As it turned out, the letter to *Pediatrics* and the response to it attracted little attention, and articles continued to appear that accepted the conclusion of both the 1997 study and my 1999 article that puberty was occurring earlier. The dissident group of endocrinologists apparently decided on another way to get their point of view before the public. They contacted Gina Kolata at the *New York Times* and told her that the pediatric endocrine community was seriously split on the issue of early puberty. Although I was interviewed by Ms. Kolata and had a chance to state my views, I will admit to being stunned when I read the article that appeared on February 20, 2001.[10] Although the letter to *Pediatrics* was signed by only eight of several hundred pediatric endocrinologists, four of those eight were quoted extensively in the *New York Times* article, whereas only one colleague other than myself (Dr. Melvin Grumbach) who supported the conclusions of the Herman-Giddens article was quoted. The dangers of assuming that girls with early puberty were normal were highlighted by providing examples of two girls whose early puberty was due in one case to a brain tumor and in another case to an adrenal disorder.

In response to the article, the Public Affairs Committee of the Endocrine Society, which represents both pediatric and adult endocrinologists, felt the need to say something about the controversy, and several in the leadership of this society were sympathetic to the views of the dissidents. They wrote a press release that the Executive Committee of

LWPES reviewed and tried to tone down a bit. However, when the press release appeared, it sounded as though LWPES was disavowing my paper, which its own Executive Committee had reviewed and approved only two years earlier. Ms. Kolata's follow-up article appeared on March 3, with the title "Two Endocrinology Groups Raise Doubt on Earlier Onset of Girls' Puberty."[11] "Two professional societies representing endocrinologists have issued a statement saying that despite the conclusion of a widely noted study, it is not yet established that girls typically enter puberty earlier today." It was suggested that further careful studies be undertaken to determine not just the average age when puberty starts but how quickly it progresses. Dr. Rosenfield stated, "This is definitely a retrenchment and a fallback to a more conservative position."

The final event in the media blitz on the puberty story took place on March 9, 2001. I had gotten a call a few days earlier from one of the producers at *Today*. After seeing the articles in the *New York Times*, they were eager to have two doctors in my field debate the issue of whether puberty was occurring earlier in girls, and had already gotten Dr. Laura Bachrach of Stanford, one of the dissenters, to fly to New York to be on the show. I was about to leave on vacation and agreed to participate on the condition that my comments could be beamed in from a TV studio in Richmond. So while Katie Couric and Dr. Bachrach sat in the NBC studio in New York, I sat in a dark, empty room at the local public TV station at 8 A.M. and waited for the segment to begin.

Ms. Couric introduced us and set the stage by stating that I believed that girls are starting puberty earlier, whereas Dr. Bachrach believed that it could be medically dangerous to assume this. Dr. Bachrach then expressed her concerns about the lack of a random selection of the subjects in the Herman-Giddens study and about the fact that since breasts were examined by inspection, fat tissue could have been easily mistaken for breast tissue. She also stated that she had seen little evidence of an increase in referrals for early puberty in her twenty-five years of practice. I countered that with seventeen thousand subjects, the chance of selection bias was very small, and that if one looked only at the 40 percent of girls whose breast tissue was palpated, the results were not very different. As to the question of why girls were maturing earlier, I emphasized the likelihood that the increased prevalence of obesity was the major factor. Dr. Bachrach countered that she thought the Herman-Giddens study was a good first effort but left many questions unanswered, including why, despite the earlier appearance of breast tissue, the mean age of menarche did not seem to have changed. She went on to say that if we accept the new definition of early puberty that I had proposed, many opportunities to find something wrong with these early-maturing girls, such as ovarian or pituitary tumors, would be missed. Finally, she stated that we needed to pay attention to the psychological distress that early puberty may cause. In my final statement, I emphasized that it was important that we educate primary-care physicians to distinguish between girls with just a little breast tissue or pubic hair but little or no progression and more serious cases with growth acceleration, rapid progression, or early menses. If we label girls who start puberty around age 8 as abnormal, I concluded, the temptation will be to put these girls and their families through hormone testing, the stress of a brain imaging study, and monthly hormone injections that might well be unnecessary.

My six minutes of airtime over, I went back to my usual routine not sure how many had seen the program, since most of the people I interact with are at work every day by 8 A.M. However, over the next days and weeks I ran into dozens of people at my job and around town who congratulated me about my appearance on national TV. Months later, colleagues, parents of my patients, and people who knew me only peripherally were still telling me how excited they had been to see me on TV. It was as though all the papers I had written over the years, all the lectures I had given, and all of the local TV news programs I had been on meant very little, but being on a nationally broadcast TV program for six minutes suddenly made me an important person. And when I think about it, I probably wouldn't be sitting at my computer writing this book were it not for a book editor seeing me on TV that fateful day in March 2001.

So what, you may wonder, has inspired a physician who spends most of his professional time seeing patients and has written an occasional article to be read by other physicians to write a book about early puberty? I will confess that the thought had never occurred to me until one day in September 2002, when a letter arrived from a senior editor at Ballantine Books asking me if I would be interested in writing a book about early puberty for parents. My first reaction was *A book? No way! How can I find enough to say on the subject to fill that many pages?* When I started thinking about it, however, I realized that most of the books and pamphlets I had seen on the subject of puberty were written to explain to kids what was happening as their bodies changed. Perhaps there was not a whole lot out there that would be of help to parents worried about whether their daughter with a few pubic hairs or a dime-sized bud of breast tissue needed to see a specialist, and if so, what the doctor might find. I had never written anything else for the general public, but I realized that I have had a lot of experience explaining the basics of early puberty to parents in my office, and I have learned over the years to explain the subject in a way that almost any parent can relate to. So I view this as an opportunity to share my acquired wisdom and usually reassuring approach to early puberty in girls with a wider audience. The good news I want to convey is that most of the girls I have seen for early puberty do not have the type of rapidly progressive precocious puberty that requires aggressive treatment. They can simply be followed by their primary-care physician at their regular well-child visits or seen once or twice by a specialist and reassured that there is little to be concerned about. Of course, it must be recognized that in a few girls early puberty can have serious consequences or may be the sign of a more serious medical disorder such as a brain tumor, but such cases are the exception, not the rule. I can say this with some confidence, because in my twenty years in practice, I have seen hundreds of girls referred for early puberty and it has been very rare that a child I thought had a benign form of early puberty proved at a later date to have something more serious. In the process, I am sure that what I write will ruffle the feathers of some of my colleagues who are convinced that early puberty in girls needs to be approached more aggressively. However, I am willing to take that chance if I can reassure some of the large number of parents who are upset and confused about what they have been told about their daughters' early development.

In the twenty years that I have been in practice, I have developed three guiding principles that apply to many of the patients I see, especially those with growth disorders and disorders of puberty. The first is that the majority of kids who are referred to specialists really have nothing wrong with them and represent variants of normal. Good specialists are skilled in identifying the minority of children referred to them who really need a full evaluation, which may include multiple blood tests, X rays, and often medical therapy. The rest of the children referred can be seen once or twice, their parents reassured, and then returned to their primary-care physicians for follow-up. An experienced physician in my field can in most cases rule out the presence of a serious condition with a good history, a focused physical exam, and a review of the child's growth chart. Not only is it costly to do lots of blood tests "just to be sure" when one has little reason to be concerned, but the lab tests often give ambiguous results, which tend to lead to more lab tests and create anxious parents. My second principle is that when it comes to costly therapies such as growth hormone for short stature and medication to suppress puberty, I think it is better to err on the side of not treating unless one is fairly confident that not treating will lead to a poor outcome or that treating will significantly improve the outcome. If I am uncertain, I will likely see the child back in six months to assess how he or she is growing and developing before making a decision. It is much better, in my opinion, to get it right, even if it takes a little longer, than to prescribe expensive medications for a child who will do fine if left alone. My third principle is that making the right diagnosis is certainly important, but if you cannot clearly explain to the family what you are thinking, you have not done a good job taking care of their child. I have seen enough parents bring their children to me for a second opinion to know how much parents value clear and straightforward explanations and having their questions answered.

What About Early Puberty in Boys?

When we discuss the trend toward earlier puberty in girls, the question inevitably arises as to whether we are seeing the same phenomenon in boys. While we do not have the same type of recent data for boys as for girls, most people in my field believe that there has been no significant shift in the age of onset of puberty in boys, and that the textbook recommendation that boys with evidence of puberty before age 9 should be evaluated is still valid. The reason is that early puberty has always been much less common in boys than in girls, and no one has reported or noticed a significant increase in cases in the last ten to twenty years. When we do see precocious puberty in boys, the chance that it is due to a more serious problem requiring treatment is greater than for girls, so most of us evaluate early-maturing boys fully. It's just that we don't need to do it very often, and thus there has been no real controversy. In chapter 5, I will present my theory as to why the trend toward earlier puberty appears to be limited to girls.

CHAPTER 1

PUBERTY 101

Whathat most parents understand about puberty is based on their own experience with it. Women typically recall the time of their first menstrual period (we use the term *menarche* when we refer to this event), and men often remember the grade they were in when they shot up four inches and kept outgrowing clothes and shoes. Some people remember puberty as a stressful time, though many of the stresses were likely more related to the difficult process of separating from one's parents and identifying with one's peers than to the hormonal changes themselves. Some mothers I have talked to who had puberty distinctly earlier than their peers recall feeling different or isolated, particularly if they went through menarche by age 10 and had no friends who had been through it before them. However, most parents I talk to do not have enough recollection of the timing and sequence of events their bodies went through between ages 10–12 and 15–17 for it to be of much help in deciding how worried to be or how to advise their children in the event one of them shows signs of puberty at an early age.

To really understand what is or is not happening when a young child exhibits signs of puberty, a basic understanding of the physical and hormonal events of puberty is very helpful. In this chapter, I will describe these events in language that is as nontechnical as possible, while setting the stage for the discussion of the mechanisms underlying early puberty in the chapters that follow. I will start with a discussion of normal puberty in girls, followed by a shorter discussion of normal puberty in boys.

THE NORMAL PHYSICAL CHANGES OF PUBERTY IN GIRLS

Breasts

In order to be sure that a girl has started to undergo puberty, there needs to be breast tissue. This sounds simple and quite obvious, but as I will explain later, it is remarkable how often this fact is ignored. In girls who have not started puberty, one can often detect a tiny amount of tissue under the nipple, the breast bud, which is usually no larger than ¼ inch in diameter. It is only when estrogen production starts to increase that the breast bud starts to increase in size. One can also see a thickening and darkening of the skin overlying the breast tissue, called the areola, and often a protrusion of the nipple at the center of the areola. Pediatricians rate breast development using the Tanner scale, developed by Dr. James Tanner. The five stages are defined as follows:

Stage 1: Prepubertal; no breast tissue present

Stage 2: Breast bud stage: a small mound of breast tissue under the nipple, slight enlargement of the areola

Stage 3: Further enlargement of the breast and areola but no separation of their contours

Stage 4: Areola and nipple form a separate mound above the level of the breast

Stage 5: Fully mature adult breast, with only the nipple projecting above the level of the breast

When puberty is in full swing, the amount of time needed to progress from stage 2 to stage 5 is about three years. However, with early-maturing girls, the progression is often slower, and as I will point out in the next chapter, very young girls can have stage 2 breast development and not progress at all for many years.

In slender or nonobese girls, simple inspection is usually adequate for a parent or a pediatrician to tell if a girl has breast development. However, in overweight girls, this is often difficult, since in the sitting position, fat over the chest can look very much like breast tissue. One clue is that when the girl lies on her back, the fat redistributes itself over a wider area and what looks like breast tissue largely disappears. The most reliable method, however, is simply palpating, or feeling for breast tissue with one's fingers. Breast tissue feels firmer and rounder than fat tissue and is located directly under the areola. My general rule is that if the diameter of the breast tissue held gently between the thumb and index finger is over ½ inch, it is likely that the breasts are starting to enlarge. However, it often takes a few months of observation to be sure.

Pubic and Underarm (Axillary) Hair

The greatest source of confusion among both parents and primary-care physicians is the meaning of the appearance of pubic hair in a young child. We are talking here about not the fine, light-colored hair similar to what may exist on other parts of the body, but dark and (if it is long enough) curly hair on both sides of the opening of the vagina and eventually above the vagina (an area called the *pubic symphysis*). We also use the Tanner scale for describing the extent of pubic hair growth as follows:

Stage 1: No pubic hair

Stage 2: Sparse growth of long, dark hairs, straight or slightly curled, along the sides of the opening of the vagina

Stage 3: Hair is darker and curlier and now spreads thinly over the pubic symphysis

Stage 4: Hair is thicker and looks like what one would see in an adult, but covers a much smaller area

Stage 5: Hair is adult in quantity and type, distributed like an upside-down triangle

It is important to understand that growth of pubic hair has nothing to do with estrogens made by the ovaries. It is due to male-type hormones made in the adrenal glands, which we refer to as *adrenal androgens*. The adrenal glands are small but vital glands that sit just above the kidneys; they also make cortisone (a hormone that is essential to life) and a salt-retaining hormone.

Because in many children pubic hair appears at the same

time as other signs of puberty, there is a widespread belief that pubic hair equals puberty. The truth is that pubic hair can appear several years before other signs of puberty (e.g., breasts) or can appear at a later time. Axillary hair is thought to reflect the same hormone changes that cause pubic hair, though in most girls detectable axillary hair will appear three to six months after pubic hair.

What regulates the ability of the adrenal glands to increase androgen production is still not clear, but we know that the hormones that stimulate the ovaries to make estrogens are not involved. In the past, most girls were said to develop pubic hair between ages 8 and 12, but more recently its appearance between ages 5 and 8 has become increasingly common.

Body Odor

Another sign thought to be characteristic of puberty is development of an adult-type body odor, originating entirely in the underarm area, or what physicians call the *axilla*. Although this phenomenon as it occurs in children has received little scientific attention, I have concluded after years of talking to parents that the development of body odor, like pubic hair, is closely related to the increase in adrenal androgen secretion. This is because the timing of the onset of body odor is usually close to the time of appearance of pubic hair. Sometimes parents report detecting the odor three to six months before any pubic hair is evident. How adrenal androgens might influence the nature of what comes out of our axillary sweat glands is not clear, nor is it clear what the role of axillary odor in human reproduction might be. It may have evolved as a way for humans to recognize when another member of the species is close to reproductive maturity.

Pubertal Growth Spurt

One of the most dramatic changes occurring during puberty is the rapid growth that typically becomes apparent within a year after the appearance of breast tissue and is directly related to increased estrogen and growth hormone production. Prior to puberty, the normal rate of growth is about 2 inches per year, but this increases to about 4 inches per year during the most rapid phase of the pubertal growth spurt. In many girls, this occurs sometime between ages 10 and 12, but there is a great deal of variability. Men may recall that when they were in fifth or sixth grade, the girls shot past them in height, only to be passed two to three years later, when the guys finally had their growth spurt.

One occasional source of confusion is when we see what looks like a growth spurt in children who are very overweight, since overweight kids often grow more rapidly than normal. However, if the breasts are not enlarging, this is not a true pubertal growth spurt.

Menarche

For years, the average age at which white girls have their first menstrual period has been about 12.7 years, though a recent study based on data collected between 1988 and 1994 suggests that this has decreased slightly to 12.5 years. In black girls, the average age of menarche is 0.4 to 0.5 years earlier, or a little over 12 years. Again, there is a great deal of variability from child to child, with some normal girls starting their periods as early as age 10 and others not starting until 15. Genetic factors are important, in that mothers who started their periods early are more likely to have daughters who start early. Another important factor is body weight and fat content. Numerous studies have shown that overweight girls have menarche earlier[1,2] and thin girls, especially thin, athletic girls (particularly gymnasts, competitive swimmers, and ballet dancers), start later.[3] In the landmark study of Marshall and Tanner, 192 white British girls were examined several times as they progressed through puberty. Published in 1969, the study showed that the average time it takes to progress from Tanner stage 2 breast development to menarche (which typically occurs at Tanner stage 4) was 2.3 years.[4] However, there is reason to believe that more recently the interval has gotten longer. One study from Spain showed that the interval from the start of breast development to menarche averaged 2.9 years in early-maturing girls but only 1.5 years in late-maturing girls.[5] Although reliable data has not been published recently in the United States, it is reasonable to assume that with girls who mature earlier, the average interval between appearance of breasts and menarche may be closer to 3 years than to 2.3 years.

The onset of menses also signals that the pubertal growth spurt has nearly been completed. Most girls grow only 1 to 4 inches after their first period, with early-maturing girls having more growth left at menarche than late-maturing girls.

THE NORMAL PHYSICAL CHANGES OF PUBERTY IN BOYS

Testicular Enlargement

It is widely agreed that the most reliable sign of the onset of puberty in boys is enlargement of the testes. In prepubertal boys, the testes measure 1 inch (2.5 cm) or less in their greatest diameter; an increase to 1¼ inches (3 cm) or more is a reliable sign that the puberty hormones of the pituitary have started to kick in. (In girls, there is a similar increase in the size of the ovaries, but since we can't measure the ovaries unless we do an ultrasound study, this change is not as helpful in assessing female puberty.) In most boys, this starts to occur between ages 10 and 13.

Pubic and Axillary Hair

Pubic and axillary hair can appear before, at the same time as, or later than testicular enlargement, because this development is driven by adrenal androgens, at least in the early stage. Thus it is not a reliable sign of the onset of puberty. In the later stages of puberty, increases in testosterone contribute to the increase in the amount of pubic hair.

Genital Enlargement, Facial Hair, and Voice Change

The growth of the penis in both length and diameter and the enlargement and reddening of the sac surrounding the testes (the scrotum) are good signs that production of testosterone is increasing. This tends to occur at least six to twelve months after enlargement of the testes is first noticeable, though there is a lot of variability in the timing.

Hair in the mustache and beard area and deepening of the voice are also changes mediated by testosterone, though they take longer to become obvious.

Pubertal Growth Spurt

This occurs on the average two years later in boys than in girls, and the average age of the growth spurt is between 13 and 14 years, usually at a time when the changes mentioned above are well established. Growth is also completed about two years later in boys, typically by age 16 or 17. It is a little known fact that most of the 5-inch difference in average adult height between boys and girls can be attributed to an extra two years of growing in boys at the prepubertal growth rate of about 2 inches per year. The *rate* of growth at comparable stages of maturation is almost identical between the sexes.

THE HORMONES OF PUBERTY

Gonadotropin-Releasing Hormone

The hormone believed to initiate most of the sequence of events described above is a tiny protein or peptide manufactured in a small part of the brain called the hypothalamus. It is made up of only ten amino acids (the building blocks of proteins) and is called gonadotropin-releasing hormone, or GnRH for short. There is a cluster of cells (called a nucleus) within the hypothalamus that releases brief pulses of GnRH about every two hours. Instead of the GnRH going into the general circulation, it is released into special blood vessels that travel down a thin structure called the pituitary stalk, which connects the hypothalamus to the pituitary gland. The release of GnRH in pulses, as I will explain elsewhere, is critical to normal reproduction. Although the sub-

TABLE 1: THE HORMONES OF PUBERTY

Hormone	Common abbreviation	Where made	Main actions
Gonadotropin-releasing hormone	GnRH	Hypothalamus	Triggers release of LH and FSH by pituitary
Luteinizing hormone	LH	Pituitary	Stimulates the gonads to produce sex steroids
Follicle-stimulating hormone	FSH	Pituitary	Stimulates maturation of the germ cells (ova and sperm) in the gonads
Estradiol	E_2	Ovaries	Stimulates growth of breast tissue and uterus; growth spurt; bone maturation
Testosterone	T	Testes	Stimulates growth of penis, pubic hair; pubertal growth spurt
Progesterone	None	Ovaries (corpus luteum)	Prepares the uterus to receive the fertilized egg and sustains pregnancy
Dehydroepian-drosterone	DHEA	Adrenal glands	Stimulates growth of pubic hair; underarm odor
Leptin	None	Fat cells	Critical level required for puberty to progress

ject of intense study (mostly using primates), the mechanism by which the pulsatile release of GnRH is largely suppressed by critical areas of the brain for all the years between infancy and puberty is still a mystery. We can be grateful, however, that nature figured out a way to restrain our species from becoming reproductively mature at a time when our brains and the rest of our bodies would not be ready to cope.

Gonadotropins

When pulses of GnRH are released into blood vessels flowing into the pituitary, they locate and bind to specific receptors on key cells in the pituitary, a bean-sized master gland located at the base of the brain and straight back from the bridge of the nose. The pituitary makes at least six different hormones, including growth hormone, but for now we will concern ourselves only with the cells called gonadotropes, because their job is to produce two key hormones, which we refer to as the gonadotropins (meaning "causing the gonads to grow"). They are called luteinizing hormone (LH for short) and follicle-stimulating hormone (FSH for short). Because GnRH is secreted in pulses about every two hours, when puberty gets under way the pituitary responds by secreting a pulse of LH and a smaller pulse of FSH about every two hours. In early puberty, it has been found that the increase in LH and FSH takes place mainly during the nighttime hours, whereas later in puberty, LH and FSH are increased all day.

Our gonads (testes or ovaries) have basically two separate but related tasks to perform, which are under the control of LH and FSH released from the pituitary gland. The job of LH is to travel to the ovaries (or testes) and stimulate the cells whose task is making the sex steroids (estrogen or testosterone). In females, FSH acts on the part of the ovaries concerned with development of the follicles that will eventually produce and nurture the eggs (called ova). In males, FSH promotes the growth and development of the seminiferous tubules, which are the factories for production of sperm. Enlargement of the testes is a reliable sign that FSH is being made to stimulate the seminiferous tubules, though it may be a while before sperm are actually produced. The proper balance of LH and FSH and the passage of several years are required for the full maturation of the gonads and the production of enough sex steroids to cause the more obvious physical changes of puberty.

An important milestone of puberty in girls is the appearance of a large surge of LH (much larger than the pulse every two hours) that triggers the release of a mature ovum from one of the follicles of the ovary, a process that is termed ovulation. This typically occurs when breast development reaches Tanner stage 4 (almost fully adult). The follicle that releases the ovum develops into a structure called the corpus luteum, which produces the key hormone progesterone. If the ovum is not fertilized, the corpus luteum regresses, and the decline in progesterone production triggers the shedding of the lining of the uterus, which results in the flow of blood we call menstruation.

Sex Steroids

In girls, the most noticeable effect of estrogens is the increase in the size of the breasts and the nipples. A less obvious but also important effect of estrogens is the stimulation of growth of the uterus and the blood vessels that line its inner surface, called the endometrium, which will play an important role in the process of menstruation. The most active estrogen, called estradiol (E_2), is also the key hormone in mediating the pubertal growth spurt. Part of this growth stimulation may involve a direct effect of estrogens on cartilage and bone, but we know that estradiol also works on the pituitary to increase the release of growth hormone. Unfortunately, it is difficult to measure how much estradiol a girl is making at a particular time, since blood levels may vary from day to day and week to week over a wide range. Physicians estimate estrogen production by looking at the size of the breasts and also at the color of the inside of the vagina. In a prepubertal girl, the color is a deep red, while under the influence of estrogens, it slowly changes to a pastel pink, and one can often see thin white mucus within the vagina.

In boys, testosterone levels start to rise within a year after enlargement of the testes is noted. Testosterone is converted to a more active form called dihydrotestosterone (DHT), and DHT causes an increase in the size of the penis, a thinning and reddening of the scrotum, and an increase in pubic hair. As mentioned earlier, testosterone causes the increase in facial hair and deepening of the voice, as well as an increase in muscle mass, though these changes take longer to develop. It is an interesting fact, discovered in the past ten years, that testosterone and DHT do not cause the pubertal growth spurt in boys, but testosterone first needs to be converted by an enzyme called aromatase to estradiol, which actually stimulates rapid growth.

Adrenal Androgens

The production of weak male hormones by the adrenal glands, referred to as adrenal androgens, starts between the ages of 6 and 9 in most girls and boys, about two years before LH and FSH start to increase; this precedes the appearance of pubic hair by about two years. The major adrenal androgen is called dehydroepiandrosterone, or DHEA, and most of it circulates in a storage form called DHEA-sulfate or

DHEA-S. Levels of DHEA and DHEA-S continue to rise until mid to late puberty and then level off. What regulates the increase in adrenal androgen production is not clear. For years, some have proposed the existence of a pituitary hormone, distinct from LH and FSH, that stimulates the adrenals to make DHEA, but its existence has never been proven. In addition, the role that adrenal androgens and pubic hair play in our species' reproductive functioning is unclear. However, we do know that individuals whose adrenal glands are not working properly (and who therefore need to take cortisone and a salt-retaining hormone in pill form) can progress through puberty perfectly well without adrenal androgens.

DHEA is the same hormone that has gotten a lot of publicity in the last ten years as a dietary supplement for adults. It has been reported to increase vigor, slow aging, and stimulate the body's immune system, but carefully done studies suggest that its benefits are modest at best.

WHAT TRIGGERS THE ONSET OF PUBERTY?

All of the glands that ultimately produce the hormones that bring about puberty are fully formed and ready for action at the time of birth. One reason we know this is that the puberty hormones spring into action in the first few months of life, a phenomenon endocrinologists refer to as the "minipuberty of infancy." It is most easy to observe in males because serum testosterone levels rise into the midpubertal range between 1 and 3 months of age, driven by increases in LH, in turn driven by pulses of GnRH. The penis and testes do enlarge somewhat, but for reasons no one has figured out, there is no pubic hair growth. By 5 or 6 months of age, testosterone levels are barely measurable and do not increase again for another ten to thirteen years. What keeps puberty in check for all those years?

It is believed that centers in the brain produce neurotransmitters that block the pulsatile secretion of GnRH, and that puberty starts when this inhibitory influence of the central nervous system relaxes. Of course, this statement just replaces one mystery with another, as no one has yet figured out what causes the inhibition to abate, but much work describing the chemical changes in the brain around the time that puberty starts in primates has been done.

Another factor believed to be important in regulating puberty is what we refer to as the hypothalamic-pituitary-gonadal axis (or HPG axis for short). It has long been known that the products of the gonads (the sex steroids and a protein called inhibin) act to suppress LH and FSH secretion in the pituitary and GnRH secretion by the hypothalamus. This "feedback regulation" is a mechanism by which most pituitary hormones are controlled, and helps prevent the hormone system from spinning out of control. It is analogous to your home heating system, in which the temperature rises to the desired range and is detected by your thermostat, which shuts the heat off until the temperature drops below the desired range. Before puberty, it takes very minute quantities of sex steroids to suppress LH and FSH, but as puberty progresses, LH and FSH increase, resulting in more sex steroids being made. The feedback sensitivity of the HPG axis is gradually reset, so that it takes progressively more sex steroids to shut off gonadotropin secretion. This alteration in feedback sensitivity allows for a tightly controlled increase in sex steroid and gonadotropin levels over a three-to-five-year period, but again, the details of how the body accomplishes this clever feat are largely unknown.

Another hormone that has recently been found to play an important role in normal reproduction is leptin, which is made in fat cells and has a critical role in regulating body weight. In mice, in which the gene for leptin was first discovered, the absence of leptin due to a genetic mutation results in the complete lack of production of LH and FSH, and the mice fail to undergo puberty unless the missing leptin is replaced. The situation is less clear-cut in humans, but we do know that in females, leptin levels start to increase at the same time that puberty hormones start to rise, and continue to increase as puberty progresses. It has been postulated that a critical level of leptin is necessary for puberty to progress in girls. I will discuss the possible relevance of leptin to earlier puberty in girls in chapter 5.

CHAPTER 2

THE DIFFERENT CAUSES OF EARLY BREAST AND PUBIC HAIR DEVELOPMENT IN GIRLS:

From the Common and Benign to the Less Common and More Serious

In clinical medicine, when a doctor is presented with a specific sign or symptom, the first task is to obtain a complete history of the problem, do a physical exam, and come up with a list of possible causes of the problem, trying to rank them from most likely to least likely. We call this process developing a *differential diagnosis*. In this chapter, I will go through, one by one, the differential diagnoses pediatric endocrinologists consider when a child who has signs of early puberty is referred to us. I will start with the two conditions we see most commonly, which are typically easy to spot at the first visit based on a history and physical exam, and progress to the more complex and serious problems, which require various blood tests and X rays to diagnose correctly.

PREMATURE ADRENARCHE
(OR PREMATURE PUBARCHE)

Over the past three years alone, I have evaluated over a hundred girls and boys with signs of early puberty, and in nearly half, the diagnosis was premature adrenarche (referred to as premature pubarche by some). What does this somewhat obscure term refer to? It is defined as *the early appearance of pubic and/or axillary (underarm) hair in a child with no other signs of pubertal development* (specifically, no breast tissue in girls, no testicular enlargement in boys). The word *adrenarche* means the increase in the production of adrenal androgens, which, as mentioned in chapter 1, stimulates the growth of pubic and axillary hair, while *pubarche* refers to the time at which pubic hair appears (in the same way that *menarche* refers to the time of the first menstrual period). These terms are used interchangeably by physicians, and I will henceforth use the somewhat more commonly employed term *premature adrenarche*.

The definition of the age at which the appearance of pubic hair is too early is somewhat controversial. The textbooks say that the appearance of pubic hair prior to age 8 in girls is abnormal, but it is so common to see pubic hair in healthy 7- and even 6-year-olds that to label these girls as abnormal is in my opinion not accurate. This is particularly true in black girls, who, several studies have shown, start growing pubic hair on average one year earlier than white girls. Suffice it to say, however, that whatever age I believe should be used as the cutoff (I think it should be 7), pediatricians refer to specialists large numbers of girls with pubic hair who are as old as 9 years. They apparently do not feel comfortable telling parents that in all likelihood these girls are normal kids who happen to have developed pubic hair a little earlier than average. It is not unusual to see pubic hair in girls as young as 5 or even 3, though it is less common at those ages than in 6-to-8-year-olds. It is my experience that in the majority of cases, parents are less worried about early pubic hair than are the primary-care physicians.

In addition to growth of hair around the genitals and under the arms, which is usually sparse but sometimes is rather bushy, the most common other finding is underarm or axillary odor. This is often noted by parents three to six months before any pubic or axillary hair appears. By the time I see these children, parents have already in most cases been applying a deodorant, which is 100 percent successful at covering up the odor and has no medical risk that I am aware of. Acne is seldom seen in these children, so if it is present, I would want to be more thorough in my evaluation to exclude another cause of early pubic hair.

The majority of girls with premature adrenarche are taller than average but are growing at a normal rate of 2 to 3 inches per year. This is reassuring, since the rare but more serious causes of early pubic hair, which I will discuss briefly later in this chapter, typically result in a rapid rate of growth (often 4 inches per year or more). I and others have found, however, that some children with premature adrenarche (15 percent in my clinic) may grow at a rapid rate and may be well above the 95th percentile in height by the time they are referred.[1] Children like this need a more careful evaluation to exclude other problems, but usually the test results will be benign, except that the bone age is advanced by two or more years (bone age will be discussed in chapter 3).

Occasionally, we are asked to see girls (or boys) who are

under 1 year old who have what is thought to be pubic hair. When it is examined closely, the hair is usually fine and of lighter color than the dark and curly pubic hair seen in older children. A couple of papers have described a small number of girls and boys with "pubic hair of infancy"; a variety of blood tests failed to turn up anything worrisome.[2,3] As long as these children are growing normally, I believe they can be watched without a lot of testing. I recently saw in follow-up a 4-year-old girl whom I had seen for this problem at age 10 months. Three years later she was in perfect health, growing normally, and the hair in the genital area was now darker and curlier, as we typically see in older girls with premature adrenarche. Thus it is quite possible that pubic hair of infancy is a variation of premature adrenarche in which adrenal androgens start to increase not long after birth.

One of the important characteristics of premature adrenarche is that the physical changes progress very slowly over time. Thus if I were to see a child with this diagnosis again in four to six months (and often I don't need to), the amount of hair will rarely have increased much. It is also unusual for other signs of puberty such as breast development to appear within six months, though clearly if one follows such girls long enough, breasts will appear.

Early development of pubic hair is not by itself harmful in any way, and there is no medical treatment that will make it disappear. My only cautionary notes are to point out that this is more likely to develop in overweight girls than in thin girls, and that studies have shown that girls who had premature adrenarche will, in their teenage years, sometimes develop worsening obesity, excess facial hair, and menstrual irregularities due to excessive androgens produced by the ovaries.[4] The term *polycystic ovary syndrome* is often used to describe this problem. If you as a parent are concerned about this problem and your daughter is overweight, the best way to prevent it is to make sure your daughter eats as healthy a diet as possible and gets regular physical activity, which will help control her weight gain.

PREMATURE THELARCHE

When a girl develops breast tissue before 3 years of age, the diagnosis is almost always premature thelarche, which we define as *the isolated development of breast tissue without other signs of puberty. Thelarche* means the time at which breast tissue appears. Close to 20 percent of the girls I have seen for early puberty over the past three years have this diagnosis. The breast tissue is usually ½ to 1 inch in diameter, and it can be either on both sides or on one side only. Most characteristically, it tends to increase little or not at all over time, and in some cases it disappears entirely. In several girls I have seen between 1 and 2 years of age, the breast tissue appeared in the first year of life; over the course of a year it neither got larger nor went away. The rate of growth in these young girls is nearly always normal, meaning that if they started at the 75th percentile, they tend to stay at the 75th percentile as they get older.

What causes this relatively common and benign situation is not entirely clear. Blood estradiol levels are usually low to undetectable but can be somewhat increased for the child's age. When girls with premature thelarche are studied by ultrasound, which is a radiation-free method for taking a picture of the pelvis, it is common to find small cysts on the ovaries, which tend to disappear over time. One theory is that these cysts, which are a normal part of ovarian development, occasionally produce estrogens for a short time and then stop doing so when the cyst disappears on its own. This brief exposure to estrogens is enough to stimulate the growth of the breast buds, but when the cyst goes away, the small amount of breast tissue persists. This would explain why, by the time the girl is seen by a specialist, the estrogen level in the blood is often so low it cannot be detected. Why we see this condition much more often before age 3 than after age 3 is unknown.

If there is any controversy about this benign condition, it concerns the question of how often premature thelarche will evolve into true precocious puberty, which will be discussed in the next section. One study published in 1988[5] suggested that about 15 percent of girls go on to develop precocious puberty when followed and tested repeatedly over time, and many physicians use this study to justify doing a lot of tests and seeing these girls on a regular basis. However, in another study from Minnesota, forty-eight girls seen with premature thelarche between 1940 and 1984 were contacted years later to see what had happened. In the majority, the breast tissue disappeared in six months to a few years, and these girls nearly always started their real puberty at a normal age.[6] I would estimate that in my twenty years in this field, I have seen over one hundred girls whom I have diagnosed with premature thelarche, and I do not recall a single one being brought back to me six months to several years later with what appeared to be true precocious puberty. So if this progression occurs at all, I believe it is rather rare.

True (Central) Precocious Puberty

This term refers to children who have all the normal signs of going through puberty but do so at a much earlier age than average (though what constitutes "average" is still the subject of debate, as will be discussed in chapter 4). Endocrinologists describe it as being an early activation of the hypothalamic-pituitary-gonadal (HPG) axis; some prefer to use the word *central* rather than *true* because this indicates that the underlying problem is in the brain or the pituitary, not the ovary. In girls, the signs that tell us we are dealing with true precocious puberty are progressive breast enlargement over at least a six-month period and an increased rate of growth: 3 to 5 inches per year instead of the normal 2 inches per year. By the time we see them, most of these girls are significantly taller than average, and are often above the 95th percentile in height on a growth chart. Pubic hair is often present, but since it reflects not activation of the HPG axis but increased adrenal hormones, its presence or absence does not really help us to decide if a girl is truly undergoing puberty. Two internal signs of pubertal progression are enlargement of the ovaries (due to increasing FSH) and enlargement of the uterus (due to increasing estrogens), both of which can be detected only if a pelvic ultrasound is done. Blood tests often show clear increases in LH, FSH, and estradiol, but there is overlap between levels seen in early pubertal and prepubertal girls, so these tests are often not decisive. A definite diagnosis may require giving an injection of GnRH before drawing the blood for LH and FSH, which I will discuss in chapter 7.

One challenge we have in evaluating girls who may have true precocious puberty is that it is often difficult to predict at the first visit which girls will progress rapidly and start menses within about two years of the appearance of breast tissue and which ones will progress more slowly or not at all over the next year or two. The slowly progressive variant of precocious puberty has been described in several studies[7,8] and appears to be fairly common. Such girls may show little change in breast size over time, display little or no acceleration of growth, and take four or more years to start menstruating. It is important to try to distinguish this form of precocious puberty from the form that progresses rapidly, because such girls, while they may need observation, will do fine without any treatment. One study showed that if the bone age was advanced by at least two years at the time of the first visit, puberty usually progressed more rapidly. Blood tests were not as helpful.

Tumors and Precocious Puberty

If we decide that a young girl indeed has true precocious puberty that is progressing rapidly, the next question we ask is what caused it to happen. For years it has been known that when we do an imaging study of the brain, such as an MRI or a CT scan, in the majority of cases we find nothing abnormal that would explain why puberty started early; these girls are said to have idiopathic precocious puberty, which means that the cause has not been determined. The observation that idiopathic precocious puberty is fairly common in 6-to-8-year-old girls and much less common in girls under age 6 has led many of us to believe that most 6-to-8-year-olds with puberty are healthy girls who are at the younger end of the broad normal age distribution for the onset of puberty. Many but not all such girls have a parent who was also an early maturer. However, we recognize that in a small proportion of girls with early puberty, we will find a tumor (or sometimes a cyst) close to the pituitary gland or the hypothalamus that is responsible. One reason a tumor can cause central precocious puberty is that it can interfere with the neural pathways from the brain to the hyopthalamus that normally suppress the GnRH neurons from increasing their activity until after age 8. The two most common tumors found in girls with true precocious puberty are gliomas and astrocytomas. Both are malignant and thus have the potential to grow rapidly and spread, but in many cases they can be removed completely or nearly completely, so a neurosurgeon needs to be consulted to figure out the best way to get it out. When part of the tumor needs to be left behind (it may be wrapped around an important structure such as the optic nerve or a key blood vessel), it is usually necessary to give chemotherapy or radiation to try to kill off the remaining tumor. However, some of these girls can be cured and have a normal life, though because of damage to the normal pituitary by the surgery or radiation, they may need hormone therapy to replace the hormones normally made by the pituitary, including growth hormone. The most common brain defect associated with central precocious puberty is not actually a tumor and is called a hamartoma. This is a developmental defect in the area of the brain near the pituitary gland and does not need to be removed because it does not grow and press on normal brain tissue. The controversial question of which girls with precocious puberty need to have an MRI or CT scan done to rule out a central nervous system problem will be discussed further in chapter 7.

The potential medical and psychological consequences of true precocious puberty are discussed in detail in the next chapter, because they are central to the controversial issue of how aggressive we should be in treating these young girls with medication to suppress puberty.

PERIPHERAL PRECOCIOUS
(OR PSEUDOPRECOCIOUS) PUBERTY

Now we arrive at a group of disorders that are more difficult to diagnose and treat but are fortunately fairly rare. The key difference is that the problem is not in the brain or pituitary (i.e., not central) but in the ovary itself, or occasionally in the adrenal glands. While in true precocious puberty, LH and FSH are increasing and stimulate the ovaries, in these cases LH and FSH are actually inhibited by sex steroids being produced in the ovaries (or rarely the adrenals). The term *peripheral precocious puberty* is starting to replace the older term because it better conveys the idea that the underlying problem is not in the central nervous system, as in central (or true) precocious puberty.

Tumors of the ovary that cause precocious puberty are very rare but can occur at any age. Growth and progression of breast development tends to be very rapid, and the tumors, which are usually benign, can grow very large. We suspect the diagnosis if initial blood tests show a very high estradiol level with a low LH and FSH. The diagnosis can be readily confirmed if a mass in the area of one of the ovaries is found on a pelvic ultrasound. Surgery is usually curative.

Occasionally an *ovarian cyst* will grow to a very large size and produce excessive amounts of estrogens. On the ultrasound exam, it will look different from a tumor, in that the mass is not solid but has fluid inside of it. While such cysts may regress if left alone, when they are very large it is common to have them removed.

McCune-Albright syndrome is a rare condition that is suspected when a young girl has breast development, irregular areas of skin pigmentation, and characteristic cystic bone changes (called *polyostotic fibrous dysplasia*). Sometimes there are spontaneous fractures of affected bone. Vaginal bleeding may be an early sign in young girls even before there is visible breast development. The ovaries are usually enlarged, with one or more large cysts. Because LH and FSH levels are low, the usual treatment for precocious puberty, which works by suppressing production of LH and FSH, does not help in McCune-Albright syndrome. Newer treatments that were originally designed for women with breast cancer and which directly inhibit production of estrogens by the ovaries or block the effects of estrogens on breast tissue and bone are being tried in this condition, with some success.

Virilizing disorders: A young girl who shows signs of excessive androgen production other than pubic and axillary hair needs to be evaluated for the possibility of an *androgen-producing tumor*. The most important changes we look for are enlargement of the clitoris, acne, and very rapid growth; occasionally we also see increased facial hair and even deepening of the voice. We say girls with such findings are showing evidence of virilization, and there will usually be an extreme increase in levels of testosterone or the adrenal androgen DHEA-S. If these levels are only mildly elevated and no tumor is found, the possibility of the inherited adrenal disorder called *congenital adrenal hyperplasia* (CAH) must be considered. Levels of DHEA-S and testosterone are increased, though not as much as with a tumor, and the appropriate blood test (which measures levels of a hormone called 17-hydroxyprogesterone) will usually lead to the correct diagnosis. Severe or classic CAH in girls is usually diagnosed in the newborn period because the genitalia are ambiguous due to enlargement of the clitoris. However, the milder or nonclassical form can present us with evidence of moderately increased androgen production anytime between early childhood and the teen years. CAH can be successfully treated with two or three daily doses of the adrenal hormone hydrocortisone.

Virilizing tumors in young girls are quite rare and can occur in the adrenal gland or in the ovary. In my career I have seen two such girls with adrenal tumors and one with an ovarian tumor. If an adrenal tumor is suspected, an abdominal MRI is the best test, while we usually look for ovarian tumors with a pelvic ultrasound to reduce the amount of radiation exposure. Both types need to be removed by a surgeon, and since they are usually benign, a cure is usually achieved.

PREMATURE MENSES

While the general message in this chapter is that the common problems are benign and the rare ones are more serious, I believe this last entity is the exception. We occasionally see a child brought in because of vaginal bleeding who has no breast development or other evidence that she is undergoing puberty, and no skin or bone evidence of McCune-Albright syndrome. The limited literature on the subject indicates that it can be seen anywhere from 1 to 8 years of age, and often there are multiple (but usually not more than four or five) episodes of vaginal bleeding, which then stops as mysteriously as it started.[9,10] While insertion by the child of an object inside the vagina can cause vaginal bleeding, it is usually accompanied by evidence of infection such as pain, irritation, and vaginal discharge. Sexual abuse should also be considered, particularly if the child is very withdrawn or has recently begun behaving abnormally. Very rarely tumors of the vagina or uterus can signal their presence in this way. However, in most cases blood tests and an ultrasound of the pelvis reveal no cause.

After seeing three cases in less than one year, I questioned my colleagues last year on our electronic bulletin board, and learned that others are also seeing this previously rare entity more often, though no one had any clue as to why. The reason for our puzzlement is that it should not be possible to have a menstrual period unless there has been a long enough exposure to estrogens to build up the lining of the uterus. However, the absence of breast tissue makes it difficult to believe that these children have been producing much in the way of estrogen. Knowing that this is in most cases a benign and self-limited process, I am now inclined to do a small number of tests and then let this mysterious problem just run its course.

CHAPTER 3

WHAT PROBLEMS RESULT FROM PRECOCIOUS PUBERTY IN GIRLS?

In this chapter, I will be discussing only true precocious puberty in young girls. As discussed in the previous chapter, except for the relatively rare cases of peripheral precocious puberty, the other diagnoses made in girls referred for early puberty represent benign conditions that progress slowly, if at all, and thus require no treatment. The problems that can occur in girls with true precocious puberty can be divided into two types, physical (mainly short stature when growth is completed) and psychological or behavioral. Although it is much easier to discuss the first issue than the second one, the behavioral issues are almost always of greater concern to parents, so I will discuss them first.

BEHAVIORAL CONSEQUENCES OF EARLY PUBERTY IN GIRLS

It is quite easy to ask what effect the early onset of puberty has on the behavior and emotional health of young girls.

However, in my opinion, nowhere else in the field of puberty research is reliable data more difficult to come by. The problem is compounded by the fact that even in girls undergoing puberty at a normal age, the effects of the hormonal changes of puberty on the behavior of girls are not exactly clear. Relatively few studies have been done to systematically address these issues, and most of those that have been done have major flaws in their design or simply included too few children to draw meaningful conclusions. There is also a tendency for both parents and physicians to impose their own biases on what they are observing in young girls who may be starting puberty at an early age. For example, if a parent is worried that early puberty is going to make his or her daughter behave erratically, the parent can usually make observations that tend to support that impression, since even perfectly normal 7-year-old girls can sometimes behave in ways that are baffling to parents. I have had several mothers emphatically use the term *PMS* to describe the moodiness they sometimes observed in their 7-year-olds, who by exam had a very small amount of breast tissue and were by any reckoning at least two years from starting menses. I will admit that child psychology is not my area of expertise, so what follows will be derived from two sources: my best attempt to summarize and interpret what has been published in this area and my own discussions with parents of young girls I have seen over a twenty-year period.

There are several reasons why early puberty in girls might cause emotional and behavioral difficulties, which I will list below with brief commentary.

1. *The physical changes of puberty (i.e., breasts) will make young girls feel different from their peers and thus cause anx-*

iety and withdrawal, as well as attract the unwelcome atten-tion of the opposite sex. The younger the girl and the more advanced her development, the more likely this is to be an issue. However, the great majority of girls I have seen for early puberty are 7 or 8 years old, and the small amount of breast tissue they have, at least at their first visit, is not visi-ble under the fairly loose clothes children wear these days. Also, as more and more girls are starting puberty early, the 7- or 8-year-old who is beginning to develop breasts is not as unusual as she would have been thirty years ago and may en-counter other girls her age going through the same changes. As for attracting male attention, the typical 7- or 8-year-old boy is pretty clueless when it comes to the opposite sex. Boys that age who do show an interest in the opposite sex (despite the teasing or ridicule they get from their peers) are usually attracted more to the face than to other parts of a girl's body.

What about the possibility that young but sexually ma-turing girls will attract the attention of teenage males or adults? I have not had parents report this to me. However, since I typically do not follow early-maturing girls long term who are not under treatment, it is possible that this is occa-sionally an issue two or three years after the onset of puber-tal development, when the breasts are large enough to be easily noticed. It is also rare to hear about young girls with early puberty who actively try to attract the sexual attention of older boys or men. Rising estrogen levels in girls just don't seem to turn on the libido the way rising testosterone levels do in young boys. In boys who are well into puberty before age 6, masturbation is a common symptom, and it is likely to be reported to physicians, since it may not be done in com-plete privacy. However, it is very rare for a parent to report self-stimulatory behavior in a young girl with early puberty.

If it were found, a behavioral rather than hormonal explanation should be considered.

2. *Girls with early puberty, being taller and more developed than their peers, may be treated by others as if they were more socially and intellectually mature than they are.* Again, this is more likely to be an issue in the small proportion of girls who start puberty very early (before age 6) and advance rapidly. Most experts agree that the cognitive development and emotional maturity of early-maturing girls is closer to that of their age-matched peers than their pubertal-stage-matched peers. However, a few studies have found that girls with early puberty had higher verbal IQs than girls the same age who had not started puberty.[1,2] This should not be a major problem in the school setting, where children are grouped by age and not size. However, outside of school, the fact that adults may misjudge the age of an early-maturing girl and expect her to be more socially mature than she is could cause frustration in the child. I suspect that this is a much less common issue than the flip side (which I hear about frequently), which is that children who are very short are quite upset when they get treated as though they are two or three years younger than they really are by people who do not know them well.

3. *Girls with precocious puberty who start their menstrual periods very early will be unprepared and suffer significant emotional distress.* Having seen several girls whose parents requested treatment for precocious puberty *after* their daughters had their first period, I think this is a legitimate concern. The age at which a young girl is prepared to deal with menses calmly (after the initial shock) has not been the subject of much study, but there is clearly a great deal of vari-

ability from child to child. It will depend a lot on the child's social maturity and adaptability, the other stresses in the child's life, and especially on how much time her mother or guardian has put into preparing her for this event. Since it typically takes two to three years from the time of initial breast development to the first period, there should be adequate time for a child to be counseled on how menstrual bleeding is a normal reproductive process and not a cause for alarm. Often the mother may not be comfortable discussing this, or the child simply may not be ready to listen.

My own impression, based on talking with parents, is that the majority of girls who start their menses before age 9 will have trouble coping even if it has been discussed with them ahead of time, while the majority of girls who have their first period at age 10 or later will manage fine. Between ages 9 and 10 it is difficult to predict how girls will cope with menses. The mother of a girl adopted from Russia who started her menses at age 9½ told me that her daughter did not understand that she had to change her pad on a regular basis. Even after nine months, she preferred to ignore it, making a mess of her clothes unless her mother kept track of when her pads needed to be changed. Girls with delayed mental and/or emotional development seem to take longer to be emotionally ready for handling menstrual flow, and many endocrinologists are more inclined to offer treatment to such girls so that the girls and their parents don't have to face this situation until the girls are older. Also, I have observed that mothers who themselves had their first period as early as age 9 often recall the experience as traumatic, perhaps because their parents had not prepared them for it. Some very good books are available for mothers to give to their daughters to help them understand the changes of puberty, including menses; these books, if presented a year or so after the onset of progressive breast enlargement, may help 9- and 10-year-olds handle this event with less stress and anxiety.*

4. *Girls with early puberty will start being sexually active at an earlier age and be at risk for earlier pregnancy.* Although this is not a concern parents have shared with me very often, I suspect that it underlies some of the anxiety that parents have about early puberty and some of the fascination that the news media have with this story. As a society, we are already worried about sexual activity starting at younger and younger ages, as well as the epidemic of teen pregnancy, and one might presume that if girls are sexually maturing more rapidly, this could contribute to this trend. Drs. Ehrhardt and Meyer-Bahlburg compared sixteen girls who had started puberty between ages 2½ and 8 with sixteen control girls who went through puberty at a normal age.[3] They found that on the average, the early-maturing girls had their first boyfriend about a year earlier than the controls and their first intercourse twenty-one months earlier, but there was considerable overlap (12½ to 16½ years for patients and 14½ to 19½ years for controls), and most of the girls with precocious puberty became sexually active at an age within the broad range of normal. When one reflects upon the extent to which young girls are bombarded by TV programs, music, and advertising of a sexual nature, one ought to conclude that any contribution of the earlier onset of puberty to ear-

Changes in You and Me: A Book About Puberty Mostly for Girls, by Paulette Bourgeois and Martin Wolfish (Kansas City: Andrews and McMeel, 1994). *The Care and Keeping of You: The Body Book for Girls,* by Valorie Lee Schaefer (Middleton, WI: Pleasant Company Publications, 1998). *Period. A Girl's Guide,* by JoAnn Loulan and Bonnie Worthen (Minnetonka, MN: Book Peddlers, 2001).

lier initiation of sexual activity is minor. As to whether earlier puberty is contributing to more teen pregnancy, that would seem even less likely in that the age of menarche has changed little over recent decades, and that age obviously sets a lower limit on when a young girl can become pregnant.

WHAT DOES PUBLISHED RESEARCH TELL US ABOUT THE EFFECTS OF EARLY PUBERTY ON THE BEHAVIOR AND ADJUSTMENT OF YOUNG GIRLS?

The best way to answer the question of what types of psychological problems occur and how often they occur in young girls who have early puberty would be to conduct this type of controlled study: A large group of girls between ages 5 and 8 with early puberty (a hundred seems like a good number to me) would be recruited from several medical centers, along with a matched control group of young girls of the same age who differ only in that they are still prepubertal. Both groups would be given a full evaluation, including a detailed medical, family, and social history, at entry into the study and a full battery of behavioral and psychological tests. The same subjects would be reevaluated yearly for at least three years, focusing on growth measurements, Tanner staging of breast and pubic hair development, hormone levels, and the battery of behavioral and psychological tests. What would make this study so valuable is that neither group would receive any treatment. Thus, over a three-to-four-year period, one could truly discover how common it is for behavioral problems to develop (or, if they were present at the start, worsen) as puberty progresses in girls who start early. By having a control group of prepubertal girls, one could easily tell if any increase in behavioral problems was really related to the early puberty, or perhaps just the social and academic pressures of growing up. Furthermore, by analyzing the data carefully, one should also be able to tell what characteristics of a young girl with early puberty at entry into the study would put her at the greatest risk for developing behavioral problems at a later time. This type of study will never be done, however, because it would be considered unethical to withhold treatment from young girls with early puberty in order to see what sorts of problems they encountered.

Some studies have been published that have examined the issue of behavioral problems in girls with early puberty, though they fall short of the ideal study outlined above. In one, published in 1985, researchers at the National Institutes of Health administered to parents of thirty-three girls with true precocious puberty the Child Behavior Checklist (CBCL), a 120-item parental report of potential behavior problems and social competence.[4] Each girl was matched to a control girl from the sample of children used to standardize the CBCL. The range of ages of the thirty-three girls was between 6 and 11 years, meaning that if age 8 is used as the definition for precocious puberty, some girls were studied several years after the onset of the problem. They found that nine of the thirty-three girls (27 percent) had a total behavior problem score of over 70; scores that high were said to occur in only 2 percent of normal girls. When they looked at specific problem areas, they found that the girls with precocious puberty scored significantly higher than controls on scales of depression, social withdrawal, psychosomatic complaints, obsessiveness, hyperactivity, and aggressiveness. So although the majority of girls studied fell within the normal range in this test, more than expected had an excess of behavioral problems. These children were studied only once, and thus we have no idea whether or not treatment to suppress the hormones of puberty actually would have improved their scores. Also, there were too few patients in the study to help decide what age and which physical or hormonal characteristics of the patients studied put them at the greatest risk for behavioral problems. Finally, there could well have been a bias in selection of patients, since they all had to travel to the National Institutes of Health in Bethesda, Maryland, to participate, and it is likely that parents who were willing to do so already had more concerns about the behavior of their early-maturing children than parents of early-maturing girls who were told about the study and decided not to participate.

A study published in 1997 from the University of Brussels in Belgium involved only twenty girls with true precocious puberty but had the advantage of using the CBCL both at the start of treatment and two years later in fifteen girls who underwent treatment.[5] At the start, all twenty girls were said to be very concerned about physical differences from peers; during treatment, five of fifteen had a significant decrease in breast size and felt less embarrassed about their pubertal development than the girls who were not treated. Feelings of loneliness decreased in the treated patients, but increased CBCL scores on the scales of withdrawal, depression, and psychosomatic complaints persisted even after two years of treatment. Thus this study tended to confirm some of the findings of the 1985 study but left open the question of how helpful treatment was in resolving the behavior problems of the young girls studied.

Another way of looking at this issue has been to study young women who had a history of precocious puberty to see how they fared from a psychological standpoint after reaching adulthood. In a study published in 1984, one group of researchers did a series of psychological tests on 17-year-old girls who had been diagnosed with idiopathic precocious puberty.[6] The only area in which they found lasting psychological effects was a tendency toward excessive psychosomatic complaints, which would include recurrent symptoms that often do not have a physical basis, such as headaches or abdominal pain, but in general the girls seemed well adjusted. In the study of Drs. Ehrhardt and Meyer-Bahlburg, differences in behavioral problems and psychosomatic complaints were also noted, but they were of a mild degree. Serious emotional problems related to the physical changes of puberty were rare and tended to occur when parents were unable to openly communicate with their daughter about her physical development. In a more recent study from Switzerland published in 2001, nineteen young women who had been treated for precocious puberty were studied by interviewing them and giving their parents the CBCL to complete.[7] Again, increased total behavior problem scores were noted, but the risk was greater for the women who ended up short as adults or who started their early puberty relatively late. The latter finding is puzzling, since the women who started puberty later than the others in the study should have been more similar to women whose puberty started at a normal age. This study lacked a control group of untreated early maturers, but the fact that an excess of behavior problems was noted even after treatment to suppress puberty suggests that early puberty might sometimes lead to long-term behavioral problems and that treatment won't prevent them. Again, I believe the study is too small to allow us to draw definitive conclusions, but it supports the notion that some girls with early puberty will be at increased risk for specific behavioral problems years later.

In summary, there is some published information to suggest that certain behavior problems are more common in girls with early puberty than in age-matched control girls, but the majority of girls with early puberty do fine in the short run and are as well adjusted as older teenagers and young adults. There is a great need for more research in this area, particularly directed at defining the risk factors for having behavior problems. I would make the prediction that girls who start puberty between ages 6 and 8 and do not progress very rapidly (a very common situation) are at much lower risk than girls who start puberty before age 6 and progress rapidly (a much less common situation).

THE RISK OF SHORT ADULT STATURE IN GIRLS WITH PRECOCIOUS PUBERTY

Although at the time of diagnosis most girls with precocious puberty are tall for their age, it has long been known that without treatment to slow rapid growth and the accompanying rapid maturation of the bones, some of these girls will complete their growth earlier than normal when they are still quite short. How do we define "short"? One way is to look at a growth chart and note that the average height for adult women is about 5 feet 4 inches, but the height of a woman at the 3rd percentile (i.e., shorter than all but three of one hundred randomly selected women) is about 4 feet 11 inches. Another way of defining "short" is to compare the height we anticipate a child will achieve with what we call the "target height." This is calculated by averaging the heights of the parents, and then adding 2½ inches for a boy or subtracting 2½ inches for a girl. Thus if the father is 5 feet 9 inches and the mother is 5 feet 3 inches, the target height of the girl will be (5'9" + 5'3"/2) − 2½" = 5'3½". Studies show that most people will end up with a height within 4 inches of their target height, so in this example, the adult height should be between 4 feet 11½ inches and 5 feet 7½ inches. Clearly, some women who end up at 4 feet 11 inches are perfectly happy and well adjusted, and wouldn't want to change anything. However, in our society, great importance is placed on height, and many parents are not happy when told their daughter might end up shy of 5 feet tall, especially if they themselves are not particularly short. This has traditionally been one of the main reasons for treating precocious puberty, since studies have shown that slowing down the rapid growth and bone maturation can allow these girls to continue to grow for a longer period of time and achieve an adult height greater than what was predicted at the time of initial evaluation. Before I discuss this further, I will need to explain what *bone age* is and how we use the bone age to predict how tall a girl is likely to be when she is done growing.

WHAT IS BONE AGE AND HOW DOES IT HELP US EVALUATE GIRLS WITH EARLY PUBERTY?

As children grow in height and weight, predictable changes take place in not only the size but the shape of their bones. These changes take place in all the long bones of the body, but when we evaluate them, we almost always do it by looking at a single X ray of the hand and wrist. Although growth and changes in shape of the hand bones have no direct impact on growth in height, we know that similar changes are taking place in the long bones of the legs and that these have a large impact on growth. It is much more convenient to take an X ray of the hand than of the foot, knee, or hip; and the hand has numerous bones whose changes over time we can examine. Over fifty years ago a book was first published that is still in use today. It was Gruelich and Pyle's *Radiographic Atlas of Skeletal Development of the Hand and Wrist*.[8] The X rays in the atlas were taken of healthy white children in the Cleveland area in the 1930s and 1940s. Children in the study were examined every three months for the first two years of life, then every six months until age 5, then annually thereafter. The atlas contains representative photographs of X rays of the hand in boys and girls between birth and 18 years of age. When we obtain a bone age on a child, what we do is put the X ray up on a lighted screen and compare it with the pictures in Gruelich and Pyle's atlas for a child of the same sex, until we find the one that matches best. You can compare the appearance of a hand X ray of a girl with a bone age of 7 (Figure 1a) to one with a bone age of 10 (Figure 1b). Most pediatric endocrinologists prefer to read bone age films themselves and do not rely on the reading of the radiologists, who sometimes do not take the same care with reading them accurately as we do. I think part of the reason is that they just have a film of a hand, and we have both a film and a patient to think about and take care of. It is not uncommon for readings to differ by a year between the endocrinologist and radiologist. The comparison method takes about five minutes and is somewhat subjective, but a more accurate method based on individually scoring

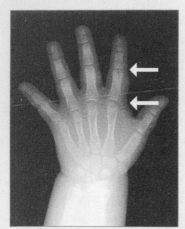 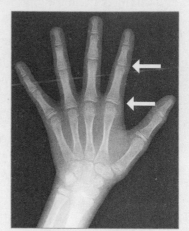

FIGURE 1a: HAND X RAY OF A GIRL WITH A BONE AGE OF 7 YEARS

FIGURE 1b: HAND X RAY OF A GIRL WITH A BONE AGE OF 10 YEARS

THE MOST OBVIOUS DIFFERENCE BETWEEN THE TWO IS IN THE SMALL BONES INDICATED BY THE ARROWS.

twenty different bones of the hand can take up to forty-five minutes to read a single X ray and is rarely used. If we are looking at an X ray and it seems to be more advanced than, for example, the 10-year standard but not as advanced as the 11-year standard, we will split the difference and call it 10½ years.

We use the bone age to predict adult height by employing tables developed by Bayley and Pinneau using the Gruelich and Pyle X rays and published in 1952.[9] What they found in studying lots of normal children is that each year of bone maturation represents a certain percent of adult height the child will ultimately reach. The more advanced the bone age, the higher the percentage of adult height the child has reached, the less growth they have remaining, and the younger they will be when they stop growing.* So a normal 7-year-old girl of average height (48 inches) who has a bone age of 7 years is estimated by the Bayley and Pinneau tables to be 75.7 percent of adult height, and from this information alone we predict an adult height of 48"/0.757 = 63.4". When the bone age is advanced by more than a year, a different table is used for "accelerated girls," which gives a lower percentage of adult height for each bone age and thus a somewhat better height prediction than would be obtained if the "average girls" table was used. This is because children with earlier puberty have a longer pubertal growth spurt, which mostly offsets the fact that they stop growing at an earlier age. If this were not the case, we would find that girls with earlier-than-average but still normal pubertal maturation would be significantly shorter as adults than girls who mature at the average age or later. Girls with precocious puberty usually have an advanced bone age at the time they are initially seen, because the sustained increase in estrogen production has a direct effect on the growing parts of the skeleton. Thus a 7-year-old seen for precocious puberty may have a bone age of 9 years, or 2 years advanced. The chart for accelerated girls tells us that with this bone age, a girl is 79 percent of her adult height. If she is of average height for her age, her predicted height would be 48"/0.79 = 60¾" = 5'0¾", at the lower end of the normal range.

---

*Many of us wonder how applicable these X rays are to children growing up sixty or seventy years later. A study published in 1993 compared X rays of over eight hundred white and black children of different ages with the Gruelich and Pyle standards. It was found that for white girls, the bone ages and chronological ages were similar, while for black girls, the bone age was advanced 0.4–0.7 years, and for white boys it was delayed by 0.4–0.9 years. How this finding impacts on the accuracy of bone age predictions is not known.[10]

However, nearly all girls with early puberty are taller than average because they have usually started their growth spurt; if this 7-year-old girl were 51 inches tall (at the 90th percentile for age), her predicted height with a bone age of 9 years would be $51''/0.79 = 64\frac{1}{2}'' = 5'4\frac{1}{2}''$, which is average for adult women and very close to the prediction for the child of average height and normal bone age. In this case, as in many I have seen, the effects of the advanced bone age and the extra height at the time of initial evaluation balance each other out, and the height prediction is normal. To illustrate this point, I have shown in Figure 2 two growth curves. The one on the right is for a girl who has breast development (thelarche) with an average height at age 10, then has a growth spurt, has her first period at age $12\frac{3}{4}$, and is pretty much done growing by age 14, achieving a normal adult height. The curve on the left is for an early-maturing girl who starts thelarche at around age 7 but is tall for her age (as is typically the case), then has an early growth spurt, followed by menarche at age 10, and then is done growing by age 12. Despite the earlier growth spurt, this girl also reaches a normal adult height, which is little different from that of the girl who started her breast development three years later.

ADULT HEIGHT IN WOMEN WHO HAD PRECOCIOUS PUBERTY

The point I am getting to is that just because a girl with early puberty has an advanced bone age, which is commonly the case, it does not by itself mean that she is going to be short. In fact, one study from the Bronx, New York, published in 1995 found that of twenty girls with idiopathic precocious puberty who did not undergo any treatment and were con-

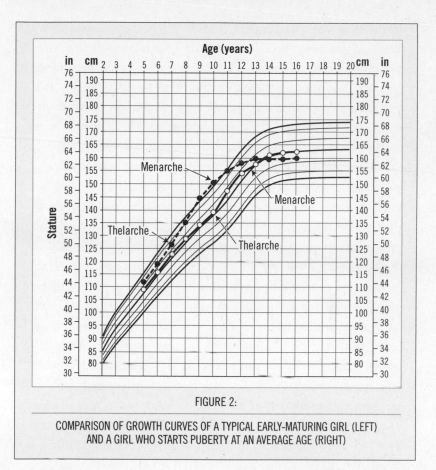

FIGURE 2:

COMPARISON OF GROWTH CURVES OF A TYPICAL EARLY-MATURING GIRL (LEFT)
AND A GIRL WHO STARTS PUBERTY AT AN AVERAGE AGE (RIGHT)

tacted when they were fully grown, 90 percent had a normal
adult height (5 feet tall or greater), and the mean height of
these twenty women was 5 feet 3½ inches.[11] One question
that comes up a lot is how accurate are the height predictions
I described using height and bone age. When one looks at a
large number of girls with precocious puberty, the agreement
between average predicted height by the Bayley-Pinneau
method and average adult height is very good, as was found

in the Bronx study mentioned above. When one looks at *individual* girls, in some cases the height is slightly overpredicted and in other cases it may be slightly underpredicted, so I tell parents that the height prediction I give them is my best guess but could be off by up to 2 inches in either direction. Other, more complex methods such as the Tanner method and the RWT method, which use other information, including the heights of the parents and the weight of the child, have been described for predicting adult height. However, studies using one of the more complex formulas show that while they may be a bit more accurate in normally-maturing girls, they really don't predict adult height as well as the simple Bayley-Pinneau method in girls with early puberty.[12]

Any study that looks at final height only in early-maturing girls seen by pediatric endocrinologists has a potential bias, since they are likely to be more different from normal than early-maturing children who were not referred. One study published in 1989 does not have this bias, and I think it gives us a pretty good idea of how much overall effect early pubertal maturation has on adult height. Adult women seen in a gynecology clinic were measured and asked to recall the age at which their menses started. Those who reported menarche at age 9 (and who presumably started breast development by about age 7) had an average height of just under 5 feet 3 inches. Those who reported menarche at age 10 had an average height of a little over 5 feet 3 inches, and those reporting menarche at ages 11, 12, or 13 had an average height of just over 5 feet 4 inches. Thus, one can conclude that women who started puberty two to four years earlier than usual had on the average a slight decrease in adult height, in the range of 1–1½ inches. Nonetheless, most achieved a normal adult height despite starting puberty early.[13]

WHICH EARLY-MATURING GIRLS ARE AT RISK FOR SHORT STATURE AS ADULTS?

I do not mean to imply that girls with early puberty never end up short if they do not receive treatment. I just want to make the point that girls who are borderline early in the age at which they start puberty (6–8 years) will most of the time reach a normal adult height without any intervention. However, girls who either start puberty before age 6 or start puberty after age 6 but progress very rapidly are at increased risk of ending up short without treatment. The reason for this is that a girl with progressive precocious puberty can have her bone age advance by two to three years per year. It is true that during this time she will also be growing rapidly, but the advancement in bone age tends to outpace the increase in "height age." A girl who is progressing through puberty at age 4 with a bone age of 6 and a predicted height of 5 feet 1 inch may, if she progresses through puberty for another two years, have a bone age of 10 or 11 by the time she has reached age 6, and a height prediction well below 5 feet. This is one reason why it is common for physicians, if they decide not to recommend treatment, to repeat a bone age test evaluation and make a new height prediction six to twelve months later. If the bone age has not advanced much more than the height age and predicted height has changed little over time, this is usually taken as a sign that puberty is not progressing rapidly. These children will generally do well without treatment, at least with respect to adult height.

Another risk factor for short adult stature is being below average in height at the time of the initial evaluation. Going back to the previous example, if the 7-year-old girl with early puberty and a bone age of 9 has a height of 46 inches, which is in the low-normal range, her height prediction is $46''/0.79 = 58'' = 4'10''$. This situation, however, does not arise as often as you might think. This is because most girls referred for precocious puberty are already having their pubertal growth spurt, and even if they were slightly below average in height at an earlier time, this spurt will bring them above the 50th percentile on the chart. However, the child who is below average when first referred to a pediatric endocrinologist for true precocious puberty will need to have a bone age and a height prediction done to help decide if she is at high risk for short stature if not treated.

In my experience, parents worry most about the behavioral consequences of early puberty, while physicians, especially those in my field, tend to worry more about adult height. To parents who are trying to adjust to their daughter's rapid growth, being told about the risk of her being short when she is finished growing is baffling, and even if they can understand the explanation, that problem may seem a long way off. While there are certainly some girls with very early onset or rapidly progressive precocious puberty who would end up quite short if not treated, this is not true in most cases. I want to reemphasize that having an advanced bone age is a normal part of being an early-maturing child and is not by itself a reason for alarm or for insisting on treatment.

CHAPTER 4

IS PUBERTY IN GIRLS
REALLY STARTING EARLIER
THAN EVER?

As you should have gathered from the introduction, the question this chapter will address has been the subject of serious and often contentious debate over the past few years. It is of critical importance in the debate over the treatment of precocious puberty, because the majority of girls whose puberty is thought to be precocious are in the borderline age range of 6–8 years. If, as I suggested in my article in *Pediatrics*, the definition of precocious puberty should really be changed from 8 years to 7 years in white girls and to 6 years in black girls, then the number of girls who truly need treatment is greatly decreased. It is also important to our understanding of human biology to know whether in fact the age at which girls start puberty has decreased over the past fifty years by as much as a year, and if so, what the most likely explanation is. It is also worth considering the evidence that black girls mature earlier than white girls and reflecting on reasons this might be so. This chapter will carefully examine the evidence available to us on whether puberty really is start-ing earlier, to help the reader come to his or her own conclu-sions, and chapter 5 will deal with the various theories as to why this might be happening.

To put this debate into a historical context, it is impor-tant to point out that evidence from several western Euro-pean countries from as far back as 1840 indicates that the average age of menarche was once 16–17 years. The clearest changes were recorded in Norway, Finland, and Denmark, and they show a steady decline in age of menarche of two to three months per decade through the middle of the twentieth century. For example, in Norway the age of menarche was 17 years in 1840, 16.3 years in 1880, 15.8 years in 1900, 15 years in 1920, 14.3 years in 1940, and 13.1 years in 1970. In the United States, a similar trend has been detected from infor-mation going back as far as 1900, when age of menarche av-eraged 14.2 years, with a decrease to about 12.6 years by 1960.[1] Additional evidence for later puberty in past centuries comes from surveys indicating that growth in a large pro-portion of individuals used to continue past the age of 20, whereas in the modern era, boys are generally fully grown by age 17 and girls by age 15.

The common explanation for this remarkable change is that improvements in nutrition and general health as well as better living conditions have been largely responsible. Until the Industrial Revolution, food supply in most of the world was rather limited, and the amount of physical labor re-quired to earn a living was considerable. Children in rural societies generally started working on the farm at a young age, and even during the Industrial Revolution, child labor was a fact of life in much of the world. Many childhood ill-nesses that are now quite rare, such as measles and tubercu-

losis, were common fifty to a hundred years ago and took
their toll on general health and nutritional status. The combination of less food and more strenuous physical activity
made for a much leaner population, just as the trend toward
greatly increased caloric intake and less physical activity
has resulted in a steady increase in obesity during the past
fifty years. Many studies done in the middle part of the last
century have shown a relationship between body fat and the
timing of growth and puberty in healthy individuals. Quite
simply, obese girls matured and had their growth spurt earlier than the average, and thin girls (especially thin and athletic girls) matured and grew later than the average. One
researcher, Dr. Rose Frisch, was so impressed with this relationship that she proposed that there was a critical weight
(or a critical amount of body fat) that needed to be attained
before a young girl could reach menarche.[2] The Frisch hypothesis was later challenged by research indicating that
factors other than body fat must also have an important effect on the timing of puberty. However, the evidence that
body fat and the timing of puberty are somehow linked remains and has been recently strengthened by the discovery
of a protein called leptin, which is made by fat cells and
seems to be important in regulating puberty. I will discuss
leptin in more detail in chapter 5.

By the middle of the twentieth century, the trend toward
earlier age of menarche appears to have leveled off, particularly in Norway, the United Kingdom, and the United
States. One study published in 1948 based on forty-eight
white girls in Ohio found the mean onset of breast budding
to be 10.8 years and the mean age of menarche 12.9 years.[3]
A study of ninety California girls published in 1953 put the
mean onset of breast budding at 10.6 years and the mean

age of menarche at 12.8 years.[4] A larger and more systematic study of puberty in U.S. girls called the U.S. National Health Examination Survey examined 2,688 girls between 1966 and 1970. The results, finally published in 1980, placed the mean age of menarche at 12.8 years for white girls and 12.5 years for black girls.[5] However, since the study only examined girls between the ages of 12 and 17, it was useless for defining the mean age at which breast development started. A 1995 study of sixty-seven white girls followed from 9.5 to 16 years of age put the mean onset of breast development at age 11.2 years.[6] It is curious, however, that the study most often quoted as defining the normal ages of puberty was not done in the United States at all, but in England. In the 1960s, Drs. Marshall and Tanner (of Tanner scale fame) decided to define the normal sequence and timing of puberty in a group of 192 white girls living in a children's home, starting at age 8 and continuing until age 18. The authors conceded that most of these girls were from the "lower socioeconomic sector" and may not have been representative of the entire white British population, let alone other racial and ethnic groups. Since the girls lived together, it was easy to examine and photograph them every three months, and Tanner staging of breast and pubic hair was determined by examining the photographs rather than the girls. Their paper, published in 1969, reported that the mean onset of breast development was 11.15 years, quite similar to what earlier U.S. studies had found.[7] The mean age of menarche in the girls was 13.47 years, which is over half a year later than what U.S. studies done around the same time had found. Nonetheless, the study was so well done that it became widely quoted as gospel in textbooks published in the United States. Their statement that "the first sign of puberty appeared between ages 8.5 years and 13 years in 95 percent of girls" became the basis for the long-standing recommendation that puberty starting in girls younger than 8 years of age be considered precocious.

One reason why the Marshall and Tanner paper was so widely quoted in the United States was that during the period from 1970 to 1990, there was simply nothing published based on U.S. populations of girls that provided meaningful data on the onset of puberty. The large study done between 1966 and 1970 could have been helpful if it had included girls as young as age 8, but for some unknown reason the people who designed the study included only girls who were 12 years or older. However, in the 1980s and early 1990s, I and many of my colleagues were seeing large numbers of girls referred for early puberty, a large proportion of whom were between the ages of 7 and 8. Many of us believed that the Marshall and Tanner data did not provide a reliable standard for the timing of puberty in American girls, but there were no more recent findings to replace it. This is the way the situation stood in 1988, when Dr. Marcia Herman-Giddens, who directed the Child Protection Team at Duke University Medical Center, published a report looking at the possible association between sexual abuse in girls and sexual precocity. She found that of 105 girls who were victims of sexual abuse at age 10 or younger, seven (one in fifteen) had evidence of sexual development before age 8.[8] When she looked in the literature to see if that was an unusually large number, she was struck by the lack of recent data from the United States on how early girls were starting puberty and whether race made a difference. She decided that she would do something to address this gap in our knowledge of the timing of puberty and started with a pilot study on signs of puberty in 3-to-10-year-old girls in North Carolina. The results convinced her that a larger study was needed and that data on white and black girls needed to be analyzed separately. She enlisted the help of a group called Pediatric Research in Office Settings (PROS for short), a program of the American Academy of Pediatrics, which helps conduct research on children being seen in the offices of pediatricians from around the country. In collaboration with PROS, Dr. Herman-Giddens wrote a proposal to collect data on pubertal status in a large number of young girls, got funding, and eventually recruited 225 physicians from sixty-five mostly suburban practices to join the study.

Participating physicians were trained to accurately stage breast and pubic hair development in 3-to-12-year-old girls who were being seen for either a well-child visit or a sick visit that would require a physical exam. The girls had their age, race, height, and weight recorded, and pubic hair and breast development were scored by inspection. Between July 1992 and September 1993, over seventeen thousand girls from sixty-five pediatric practices around the country who were part of the PROS network were examined and their sexual development rated. About 90 percent were white and 10 percent were black, similar to the proportions in the whole U.S. population. It took an additional three and a half years for the statisticians to analyze the data; then the paper was written, revised several times, submitted for publication, revised again, and finally published in the April 1997 issue of *Pediatrics.*[9]

The key findings of this landmark paper are shown in Figures 3 and 4. The girls were categorized by age and race, and as seen in Figure 3, a remarkable 37.8 percent of black 8-year-olds (defined as from their eighth birthday to the day before their ninth birthday) and 10.5 percent of white 8-year-olds had already begun breast development. An equally impressive 34.3 percent of black and 7.7 percent of white 8-year-olds had begun pubic hair growth. (I need to emphasize here that although pubic hair is not the same as puberty, it is quite striking that the apparent trend toward earlier breast development has been paralleled by a very similar trend toward earlier appearance of pubic hair.) The average age of onset of breast development was estimated to be 10 years for white girls and 8.9 years for black girls, while for pubic hair, the figures were 10.5 years for white and 8.8 years for black girls. Since the group of 8-year-old girls had an average age of 8.5 years, for the paper I wrote for *Pediatrics* I estimated the percentage of girls with breast development by age 8 by averaging the percentage for 8-year-olds with the percentage for

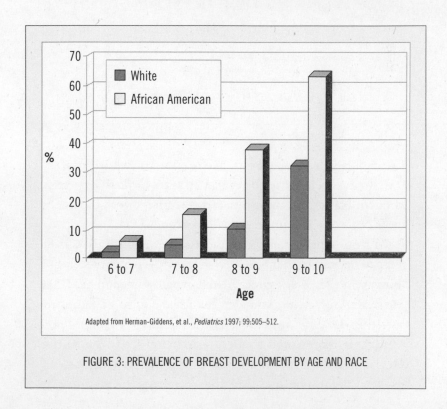

Adapted from Herman-Giddens, et al., *Pediatrics* 1997; 99:505–512.

FIGURE 3: PREVALENCE OF BREAST DEVELOPMENT BY AGE AND RACE

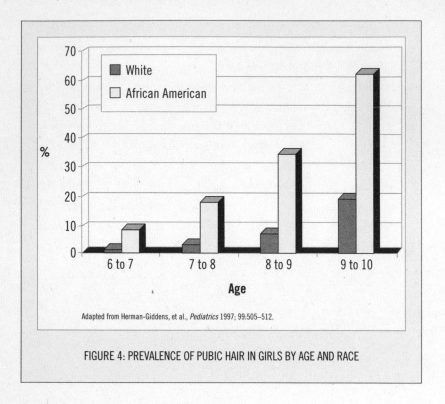

Adapted from Herman-Giddens, et al., *Pediatrics* 1997; 99:505–512.

FIGURE 4: PREVALENCE OF PUBIC HAIR IN GIRLS BY AGE AND RACE

7-year-olds, who had a mean age of 7.5. For white girls, the estimated percentage with breasts by age 8 came to 8 percent, while for black girls, the estimated percentage with breasts by age 8 came to a still impressive 26 percent.

Curiously, the mean age of menarche for white girls, 12.88 years, was close to that reported in the 1980 paper mentioned above, while for black girls, the mean age of menarche, 12.16 years, was somewhat younger than the 12.5-year figure reported in 1980. It was clear that the findings for breast and pubic hair represented a major departure from the British data of Marshall and Tanner and from the very limited earlier U.S. data. The question that occurred to many upon reading this article was: Were the data reliable or flawed, and should they result in changes in how we define precocious puberty in girls?

As mentioned in the introduction, I was given the task by the president of the Lawson Wilkins Pediatric Endocrine Society of reviewing the Herman-Giddens study. One issue that needed to be addressed was whether the results obtained on the seventeen thousand girls were representative of the U.S. population as a whole. While no effort was made to select the subjects in a truly random fashion, it seemed to me that the study was large enough that a significant bias was unlikely. The PROS practices that enrolled subjects were mostly suburban, but there was no reason to believe that the proportion of early-maturing girls would be higher in inner-city or rural practices than in suburban practices. It seemed unlikely, as some have proposed, that mothers of early-maturing girls were more likely to bring their daughters in for a well-child visit because of a concern about their breast or pubic hair development that they were reluctant to reveal. Although parents could refuse to have their daughters participate in their pediatricians' research, less than 1 percent of eligible girls who visited a participating office while the study was in progress were not enrolled.

The biggest concern I had about the study was that breast development was assessed by inspection, not by palpation, since sometimes it is difficult to distinguish fat from real breast tissue, especially in overweight girls. When I asked Dr. Herman-Giddens why the study did not require that breasts be examined by palpation, she said she wanted the results to be comparable to all the other studies (many mentioned in this chapter) based on Tanner staging, which by definition is done by visual inspection only. She did allow the doctors to record their impression of the breast stage by palpation if they wished, and 39 percent did so, but only the data obtained by visual inspection were used for the final publication. I therefore asked the statistician for the PROS study to compare the results recorded by inspection with those recorded by palpation for the 39 percent of girls who had breast development rated by both methods. It turned out that 4 percent of girls with breast development by inspection had no breast tissue by palpation, while 1.7 percent of girls who had no breast development by inspection were found to have breast tissue by palpation. In other words, in the great majority of cases, the inspection and palpation rating of breast development agreed. To see if possible errors in rating breast development were much more common in overweight girls than in thin girls, we compared the most overweight 25 percent of girls (based on body mass index, calculated from weight and height) with the thinnest 25 percent. In the overweight group, 15 percent had breast tissue by inspection but not palpation, while in the thin group, 13 percent had breast tissue by inspection but not by palpation. Thus the occasional misclassification of fat tissue as breast tissue was just as likely to occur in thin girls as in fat girls. Finally, we considered the possibility that the dramatic increase in the percentage of girls with breast development between the ages of 6 and 10 could be explained by the older girls being significantly fatter than the younger girls. However, within that age range, a stable 14–15 percent of white girls and 21–28 percent of black girls had a body mass index above the 90th percentile for their age. I interpreted these findings as evidence against the hypothesis that the higher-than-expected percentage of girls with breast tissue before age 10 could be explained by errors on the part of the examiners in confusing fat tissue with breast tissue. While it would have been ideal to do visual scoring and then palpation for *all* the subjects, the data above suggest that the results of the PROS study were not significantly altered by relying on inspection as the primary method of examining breasts.

Support for the conclusions of the Herman-Giddens study has come from another study done at approximately the same time. Between 1988 and 1994, the federal government sponsored a new study called the National Health and Nutrition Examination Survey (third cycle), called NHANES III for short. In this study, seven thousand subjects between ages 1 and 16 were scientifically selected to be representative of the population as a whole, but the proportion of black and Hispanic boys and girls studied was intentionally greater than in the whole population to make comparisons between white, black, and Hispanic children easier. Both growth measurement and pubertal staging were done for the 1,623 girls between ages 8 and 16. Breast development was assessed by inspection, as in the PROS study.[10] Table 2 shows the percentage of 8-year-old girls with breast and pubic hair development, comparing the PROS study and NHANES III. It confirms that breast and pubic hair development in 8-year-old girls is common, especially in black girls. There were not enough Hispanic girls in the PROS study to provide data on their pubertal development, but in NHANES III, Hispanic girls, like black girls, show a high prevalence of breast development by age 8, but their prevalence of pubic hair at age 8 is closer to that of the white girls.

When the mean age of breast and pubic hair development is compared for the two studies (Table 3), the similarities are again obvious.

What I conclude from these numbers is that the finding of

TABLE 2: COMPARISON BY RACIAL/ETHNIC GROUP OF PREVALENCE OF BREAST
AND PUBIC HAIR IN 8-YEAR-OLD GIRLS FROM THE PROS AND NHANES III STUDIES

	% with breast development		% with pubic hair development	
	PROS study	NHANES III	PROS study	NHANES III
White girls	10.5	11.4	7.7	6.5
Black girls	37.8	27.8	34.3	30.4
Hispanic girls	—	25.4	—	6.7

earlier onset of puberty in the PROS study was not an aber-
ration due to nonrandom selection of subjects, but was confirmed by another study done around the same time with a
more scientific method of patient selection.

A recent analysis of the NHANES III study also shows
that the mean age of menarche in 1988–1994 was in fact
slightly earlier than what was reported for the NHES study
done in 1966–1970: 12.54 years versus 12.75 years.[11] To put it
another way, the recent NHANES data show girls starting

TABLE 3: COMPARISON BY RACIAL/ETHNIC GROUP OF THE
MEAN AGE OF APPEARANCE OF BREAST AND PUBIC HAIR
IN 8-YEAR-OLD GIRLS FROM THE PROS AND NHANES III STUDIES

	Mean age of onset of breast development		Mean age of onset of pubic hair development	
	PROS study	NHANES III	PROS study	NHANES III
White girls	10.0	10.3	10.5	10.5
Black girls	8.9	9.5	8.8	9.5
Hispanic girls	—	9.7	—	10.3

their periods about two and a half months earlier than twenty years before. This may not seem like a big difference, but if the trend was to continue, the average age of menarche would decrease by over a year in the course of a century.

Indirect additional evidence for earlier puberty also comes from the Bogalusa Heart Study. Between 1973 and 1992, seven different studies were completed in which 3,000–3,500 children between the ages of 6 and 16 were carefully measured. In 2000, an analysis of growth patterns was published that looked for trends in growth over a nearly twenty-year period in black and white boys and girls.[12] What emerged was a pattern in which between ages 10 and 12, the 1992 children were almost an inch taller than their 1973 counterparts, but by age 18, they were no longer any taller (in fact, the white girls were somewhat shorter). The simplest explanation for this finding is that children in 1992 were starting puberty and having their growth spurts earlier, resulting in their being taller at 10–12 years of age but not ending up any taller when growth was completed. An additional analysis of this study published in 2002 showed that over a twenty-year period, white girls began having their periods two months earlier in the 1990s versus the early 1970s, but for black girls, the trend was for menses to start nine months earlier.[13] Although this study looked at young girls in only one area of one state and was not a nationally representative sample, it supports the notion that puberty in girls is starting earlier now than in the recent past.

ARGUMENTS AGAINST THE EARLIER
ONSET OF PUBERTY IN GIRLS

To summarize, we now have three fairly large studies of young U.S. girls, done around the same time, showing that a significant proportion of girls, especially black girls, are developing both breasts and pubic hair at an age the textbooks tell us is too early or "precocious." So why, you may ask, do a vocal minority of pediatric endocrinologists insist that the evidence that puberty in girls is starting earlier is inconclusive and that no changes in the recommendations as to when puberty is too early are warranted? This has puzzled me a great deal, since many of these physicians practice in areas with large black populations, and they should presumably be seeing the same trends that I and most of my colleagues have noticed. One reason they have given is that perhaps the age of developing breasts and pubic hair twenty to thirty years ago was already earlier than what the textbooks tell us, but since there were no puberty studies done at that time in the United States, there are no good data for comparison, so we can't really say that a trend for earlier puberty exists. My reply to this objection is that there is nothing at all that we can do now about the unfortunate lack of good studies on the age of puberty in U.S. girls before 1990. However, it makes little sense to continue to use the data of Marshall and Tanner to guide us in deciding what is average and what is too early for contemporary U.S. girls. After all, that study was extremely nonrandom, looking at only white girls living in the same group home in 1960s England. In light of the more recent data, it makes much more sense to view 7- and 8-year-old white girls and 6-to-8-year-old black girls with signs of puberty as largely being healthy girls who are at the tail end of the normal distribution of the timing of puberty.

Another argument used to cast doubt on the validity of the PROS study is that since the average reported age of menarche is close to what was found thirty years earlier, the earlier onset of breast development could not have occurred unless the speed of progression, or tempo, of puberty is slower now than in the past. While some in my field find this implausible, most of us have no problem with the concept that the tempo and duration of puberty could be changing over time. As mentioned in chapter 1, a study from Spain showed that the duration of puberty (from breasts to periods) averaged 2.9 years in early-maturing girls but only 1.5 years in late-maturing girls. Is it that surprising that with more girls starting puberty at earlier ages, the time needed to progress through puberty might be greater than in the past, when the average interval between breasts and menses was just over two years? Unfortunately, there are no recent data (like that Marshall and Tanner published in 1969) in which a large number of U.S. girls have been studied as they progressed through puberty. However, there are reports of girls with the slowly progressive form of precocious puberty in which some individual girls took as long as four years after breast development to start their periods. Furthermore, recent analysis of the NHANES III data and the Bogalusa Heart Study, as mentioned earlier, indicates that the average age of menarche has actually declined over a twenty-year period, by about two months overall, and by as much as nine months in black girls.

The argument that the PROS study is flawed because the subjects were not selected at random and thus are not representative of the U.S. population was discussed earlier and seems a bit of a stretch considering how many girls were studied. In addition, the lack of a random sample of girls was not a problem with NHANES III, in which scientific methods were used to select a population that was representative of white, black, and Hispanic girls in the country as a whole. As for the argument that the study is unreliable because of the potential for mistaking fat tissue for breast tissue, I have described why I think this is very unlikely to have distorted the findings of either the PROS study or the NHANES study in a major way.

Several physicians in my field who are uncomfortable with revising the puberty guidelines believe that even if puberty is occurring at an earlier age, that does not make it "normal." I would agree that having girls start puberty as early as 7 or 8, though it appears to be increasingly common, is not a very desirable trend. However, I believe this trend will be with us for a long time, whether we like it or not, for reasons I will discuss in chapter 5. If we simply refuse to accept this reality, we will need to provide referrals and full endocrine evaluations for a significant proportion of our young girls. Furthermore, many endocrinologists will feel an obligation, once they have concluded that a young girl has started puberty, to treat her with expensive medications in order to prevent what are thought to be the serious physical and emotional consequences of early puberty. As I pointed out in chapter 3, these consequences may be real in a minority of early-maturing girls but are overstated for the majority. If this trend continues, society will have to adapt. Parents may need to prepare their daughters for starting to menstruate earlier than they did in the past, and sex education may need to start a year earlier in schools. However, 7-year-old girls with breast development will be more likely to have a few friends who are going through the same changes, so there may be fewer problems in the future with these girls feeling different or isolated.

The most emotional argument made for not changing the guidelines for when puberty is too early is that to do so would greatly increase the risk of overlooking children with serious problems who would have been discovered and treated properly if only their primary-care physician had referred them to a specialist. The story in the *New York Times* made much of the fact that the physicians interviewed knew of at least two children who were thought to be normal early maturers based on the revised puberty guidelines but were eventually found to have conditions requiring evaluation and treatment. One proved to have a brain tumor and one had a rather uncommon form of congenital adrenal hyperplasia (as mentioned in chapter 2, this is a condition where the adrenal glands, due to a genetic mutation, overproduce adrenal androgens). In their letter to *Pediatrics*, the dissident group of pediatric endocrinologists wrote that "liberalizing the definition of normal carries the risk of overlooking pathology," and they concluded that "when breast or pubic hair appear before age 8 or 9 years, respectively, regardless of race, we are of the opinion that a diagnostic evaluation should be initiated with evaluation of bone age and height prediction." Thus the authors of the letter would prefer that physicians continue to refer to specialists the substantial proportion of white girls and the significantly higher proportion of black girls, who, according to the results shown in Figures 3 and 4 and Table 2, would be expected to start breast development or pubic hair development by age 8. Whenever we "liberalize the definition of normal," we always slightly increase the risk of overlooking a serious problem, but that is a common and necessary trade-off in the field of medicine. Published guidelines for when a problem is serious enough to be referred for further evaluated need to be updated from time to time as new information becomes available; it is part of the process of trying to make medical care cost-effective. For example, recent studies show that for children being seen in an emergency room for head trauma, one can avoid doing brain imaging studies on a large proportion without missing anything if certain guidelines based on the history and the physical exam are followed. In addition, physicians should be trained to assess which patients with the same complaint are at the greatest risk for having something serious going on, and decide how much testing to do according to that risk. I believe that if we did a better job training pediatricians to recognize the signs suggesting that a girl with early puberty needs a full evaluation by an endocrinologist, the risk of missing a serious problem would be acceptably low.

The letter to *Pediatrics* also included the statement that "we are of the opinion that a well-designed study is necessary before a conclusion can be drawn about the normal age of puberty." As mentioned in the introduction, after the article in the *New York Times*, one of the key items in the Endocrine Society's press release was the call for more research on the subject of early puberty in girls. While I have no objection to this, it occurred to me that even if someone such as myself had the time and energy to do the perfect study, the time it would take to design the study, apply for funding, get the funding, recruit the sites (doctor's offices or schools) where the girls would be examined, obtain approval for research involving human subjects, train the examiners, collect the data, analyze the data, write the paper, get it reviewed and revised, and finally see it published would be eight to ten years! So as I see it, we have two choices. One is to view the PROS and NHANES III studies as the best that have been done to date and incorporate their findings into the way we practice. The second is to ignore these studies and wait indefinitely for a better one to be published, while continuing to use as the standard for the normal timing of puberty the 40-year-old Marshall and Tanner study. I believe that the majority of physicians in my field agree that the old guidelines, which view girls who mature earlier than 8 years of age as abnormal and at high risk, are outdated, and that the new guidelines better reflect the reality of what is happening in contemporary U.S. girls.

CHAPTER 5

IS IT IN THE ENVIRONMENT
OR IN OUR FAT CELLS?

T he controversy over early puberty in girls involves more than just the question of whether girls are really going through puberty earlier today than twenty or thirty years ago. When people hear about girls commonly starting puberty at age 7 or 8, many of them want to find a culprit, and the media reports of this story have been full of theories that blame the phenomenon on a variety of chemicals in food and the environment. The first part of this chapter will review the evidence that has been cited in favor of these theories, and then I will discuss what I and most of my colleagues think is the real culprit: the increase in childhood obesity. I will also address the question of why black girls are starting puberty approximately a year earlier than white girls.

For better or worse, we live in a society in which many people are convinced that any observed negative trend in our health can be related to some chemical or radiation exposure in the environment. Some of these concerns clearly have merit, such as the increase in cases of leukemia and certain types of cancer in parts of the country where there is strong evidence of contamination of the water supply by chemicals produced and released by specific companies located in the vicinity. Some of the more celebrated cases were recounted in books and movies, including *Erin Brockovich* and *A Civil Action*. In other cases, extensive epidemiological studies have failed to support a connection between environmental exposure and disease. Two good examples are living close to power lines, which does not appear to increase the rate of leukemia and other cancers, and mercury-based preservatives in childhood vaccines, which several large studies indicate are not linked to autism. I hope to show that although there are several intriguing theories that link chemical exposure to early puberty in girls, in no case do we have strong evidence that such exposure can account for the nationwide trend documented in the previous chapter.

ESTROGENS IN MEAT AND POULTRY

There have been two epidemics of early puberty that are suspected to have been caused by exposure to estrogens in food, specifically meat and poultry. You will recall that estrogens, a type of hormone normally made by the ovaries, cause both breast development and the pubertal growth spurt in girls. If young children were to consume meat products contaminated by estrogens fed to the animals to fatten them up, a large number of cases of early breast development would be observed in a small area over a relatively short period of time. The first reported outbreak of early breast development took place in girls in Italian schools between 1977 and 1979.[1] In a single school in Milan, several hundred children were affected. Although a source of estrogen was never identified, it was suspected that an unregulated supply of poultry and veal was the source of the problem. As investigations of estrogenic contamination of meat were getting under way, the problem subsided. A more widely studied epidemic took place in Puerto Rico between 1976 and 1984. During this time, on an island with a total population of about three million, 482 girls were identified with premature thelarche, about 60 percent of whom were under 2 years of age.[2] Elevated levels of estrogens were found in the blood of about 30 percent, but few had elevated levels of LH and FSH, suggesting this was not truly central precocious puberty caused by an early increase in pituitary gonadotropins. A few samples of milk, chicken, and pork were tested for estrogenlike substances, and one of the chicken samples showed very high levels, but the exact substance was never identified. Close to 60 percent of the children who had developed breasts and were taken off locally produced milk, chicken, and beef had disappearance of the breast tissue within two to six months. By 1984, the number of cases of premature thelarche was declining sharply. It was noted at the same time that the weight of chickens brought to market declined, adding to the suspicion that local farmers had added hormones to the poultry to increase yields and then stopped when their practices came under investigation.

In the United States and in Europe, the hormone content of meat and meat products is monitored, and the FDA defines an intake of up to 1 percent of the normal daily estrogen production rate in prepubertal children as safe. How accurate these measurements are is debatable, and it is certainly possible that chronic low-level estrogen exposure from meat products occurs in U.S. children. Also, it is not clear if the industry has conducted any research on the subject. However, no localized outbreaks of early breast development have been reported in the continental United States, which would likely be the case if farmers in a specific area were trying to fatten their chicken or beef with generous supplements of estrogens. Two of the experts in this field, Drs. Paretsch and Sippell of Kiel, Germany, recently concluded that "there are no published data to support the notion that an increased overall exposure to environmental estrogens has led to an increased incidence of precocious puberty."[3]

ESTROGENS IN COSMETICS AND HAIR CARE PRODUCTS

Another potential source of estrogenic exposure in young children is by contact with skin. There have been several published reports of young girls with breast development which was most likely due to estrogen-containing skin care or hair care products used by them or their mothers. Hair care products containing either estrogen or placenta (extracts of which contain estrogens) are typically sold not in grocery stores but in establishments emphasizing natural ingredients. One study found that 8 percent of girls with sexual precocity in a military clinic in Maryland had used hair care products containing estrogens or placenta.[4] The authors also pointed out that 64 percent of black women used such hair products, and raised the possibility that young girls can become indirectly exposed to estrogens through contact with their mothers' hair, so the magnitude of this problem hasn't been well defined.

ENDOCRINE DISRUPTERS IN
THE ENVIRONMENT

A large body of evidence has accumulated in recent years that a variety of manufactured compounds being released into the environment have the potential to interfere with human reproductive function. In certain tests conducted mainly in animals, these chemicals have been found to mimic the effects of estrogens, block or antagonize the effects of estrogens, or antagonize the effects of androgens. Whether they are present in our bodies in sufficient quantities to have harmful effects is still a matter of controversy, but because of their *potential* to disrupt normal reproductive processes, they are referred to as "endocrine disrupters." I will focus on those studies in which investigators have specifically looked at the effects of some of these substances on growth and puberty of children, steering clear of the debate over whether they can be linked to such trends as increasing rates of breast cancer in women and decreasing sperm counts in men.

Attempts to link early puberty to exposure to endocrine disrupters are complicated by the fact that the event being observed (onset of puberty) may be occurring many years after exposure to the chemical in question. It may be of little use to measure blood levels of a pesticide-related chemical in an 8-year-old girl if the critical exposure that may have altered the timing of puberty took place during fetal life or around the time of birth. There is one very good study, however, published in 2000, that collected information on exposure to these chemicals at the time of birth and related it to the timing of puberty fourteen years later.[5] Researchers at the National Institute for Environmental Sciences in North Carolina were interested in two environmental contaminants: DDE, which is a breakdown product of the insecticide DDT, and polychlorinated biphenyls (PCBs), which were used in many manufacturing processes including production of electrical equipment. Based on animal studies, these chemicals have been reported to have a variety of effects on reproduction, including accelerated puberty in female rats. Neither DDT nor PCBs have been manufactured since the 1970s, but they break down very slowly, so they are still in the environment, and DDE can still be detected in most people today. In 594 boys and girls initially studied between 1978 and 1982, PCBs and DDE were measured in breast milk, maternal blood, umbilical cord blood, and the placenta to estimate exposure both across the placenta prenatally and through breast milk postnatally. Starting in 1992, when the oldest children in the study were 14, researchers contacted them once a year by mail and asked the family to report height, weight, and their stage of puberty. When all children had completed puberty, the authors tried to relate growth and mean age of reaching different stages of puberty in boys and girls with different levels of PCB and DDE exposure around the time of birth. In brief, there was no effect of either PCB or DDE exposure on the timing of puberty in either sex. However, boys with the highest prenatal exposure to DDE were somewhat taller and heavier at age 14 than those with the lowest exposure. Although this study by no means eliminates the possibility that prenatal and neonatal exposure to PCBs and DDE may have subtle effects on growth and development of children, it does not offer support to the theory that the trend for earlier puberty in girls in the 1990s can be related to these environmental chemicals.

Another study published in 2000 has kept this area of investigation very much alive.[6] Researchers in Michigan followed a group of mothers and their children who were among four thousand individuals exposed in 1973 to an accidental contamination with polybrominated biphenyls (PBBs), which are close cousins of PCBs. They estimated prenatal exposure to PBBs by measuring maternal blood levels three to six years later. The key finding was that breast-fed girls who were exposed to high levels of PBBs before birth had an earlier age of menarche (11.6 years) than non-breast-fed girls (12.7 years), and earlier pubic hair growth. More relevant to our discussion was that there was little association with breast development. Even if they had found earlier breast development in the more heavily PBB-exposed girls, to say that this supports an environmental cause of earlier puberty in girls would be a bit of a stretch. This was, after all, an unusually heavy exposure taking place in a restricted area of one state.

Researchers in Belgium have examined the possible connection between pesticide exposure and early puberty in girls. In several European countries where large numbers of children have been adopted from developing countries, an unusually large number of girls with precocious puberty has been seen. It was initially postulated that a combination of genetic factors and the transition from an underprivileged and undernourished environment to a privileged environment could account for the early maturation. A group of Belgian investigators, however, decided to investigate the possibility that prior exposure to DDT, measured as its breakdown product DDE, might be implicated.[7] They found that both foreign adopted and foreign nonadopted girls with precocious puberty (who came mostly from Latin America,

Africa, and Asia) had serum levels of DDE well above the largely undetectable levels found in native Belgian children with precocious puberty. The authors speculated that DDE, being a weak estrogen, might act in the brain to promote maturation of the hypothalamus and eventually the entire HPG axis, resulting in central precocious puberty. The major problem with this study, however, is the lack of a suitable control group. The results could easily be explained by Belgium having a much lower level of environmental contamination with DDT than the developing countries from which the young girls came. The proper control group would have been age-matched girls from developing countries who had no evidence of early puberty, but they were not studied, probably because they had no reason to visit the group of pediatric endocrinologists who did the study.

Another group of chemicals that has been found to have estrogenic activity is the phthalates, which are used in the manufacture of plastics. In a recent study from Puerto Rico, serum samples were analyzed for phthalates in forty-one girls with onset of breast development between ages 6 months and 8 years and compared with thirty-five control samples. The authors reported that 68 percent of the girls with premature thelarche had high levels of phthalates, compared to only one control girl (3 percent).[8] This suggests that at least in Puerto Rico, environmental contamination with phthalates could be an important cause of early breast development. Although phthalates have been found to be widespread in the environment, no comparable data from the continental United States has yet been reported.

The message I have taken from these studies is that while there are some interesting findings that need to be explored further, there is no compelling evidence that the trend for earlier puberty can be traced to endocrine-disrupting contaminants in the environment. Even if one could point to a situation where a localized and defined high level of chemical exposure was related to earlier breast development, it would be very difficult to generalize that finding to what appears to be a nationwide trend toward earlier puberty in girls. We should also reflect on the fact that DDT and PCBs have been around for decades but have not been manufactured since the 1970s due to health and safety concerns. Although they have persisted in the environment, exposure of our entire population over time should be decreasing, not increasing. Thus it is difficult to see how the trend for earlier puberty, which most of us believe has occurred between the 1960s and the 1990s, would be happening at the same time as the DDE and PCB environmental burden has decreased, if the two events were related.

FAMILY RELATIONSHIPS, STRESS, AND EARLY PUBERTY

As mentioned in the introduction, an article in the *New York Times Magazine* in December 2000 discussed the work of a psychologist named Jay Belsky, in the context of the debate over possible causes of early puberty. In 1991, Belsky proposed a theory that predicted that girls raised in a very stressful home environment would start puberty earlier, start childbearing earlier, and bear more children, but invest less time and energy in raising them than girls with more harmonious family relationships in early childhood.[9] (Intuitively, it makes as much or more sense to predict that stress would *delay* puberty and childbearing, since survival of the species is promoted by not just more offspring, but offspring who are well cared for and survive into adulthood.) At least two groups of researchers have conducted studies testing this prediction. One researcher reported a short-term study of eighty-seven adolescent girls examined over a period of several years, which found that the father's presence in the home and more father-daughter affection predicted later timing of puberty in girls who were in the seventh grade.[10] In girls who were not living with their biological fathers, the presence of a stepfather rather than the absence of the father appeared to have the strongest relationship to earlier pubertal maturation. A recent study from Poland looked at the age of menarche in over two hundred girls from families free of major trauma compared to sixty-four girls whose family dysfunction exposed them to major and prolonged stress.[11] It was reported that the mean age of menarche in girls from the more stressed families was 12.9 years, about 0.4 years earlier than the girls from the nonstressed families, in which it was 13.3 years (it appears that Polish girls are somewhat later than U.S. girls in their mean age at menarche).

Based on these two recent studies, I think that it is entirely possible that Belsky's theory of psychological stress triggering earlier puberty in young girls has some merit. Some geneticists have suggested that genetic factors, not stress, could account for the association between distant fathers and early-maturing daughters, since fathers and daughters share half their genes. Clearly more research needs to be done in this area. While I won't dispute that girls who live with their stepfathers may start puberty earlier than girls from intact families, the question of whether it explains why girls are maturing earlier now than thirty years ago is another matter. Dysfunctional families, high rates of divorce, and blended families have been with us for a long time. According to the National Center for Health Statistics, the divorce rate, which was fairly constant during the 1950s and early '60s, rose sharply from 1966 to 1976, leveled off, and then began to decline slightly after 1981.[12] One would think that if an epidemic of divorce and living with stepparents were driving the trend toward earlier puberty in girls, a continued rise in the divorce rate would have been apparent in the last quarter of the twentieth century. It is possible that the rise in out-of-wedlock births may also need to be factored into the equation. Dr. Herman-Giddens shared with me the fact that such births in the state of North Carolina increased from 19 percent of births in 1981 to 34 percent in 2001, and the rates were much higher for black girls than for white girls. Many girls born out of wedlock are raised in homes without their fathers, so this is another area that needs further investigation.

EARLIER PUBERTY AND THE TREND TOWARD INCREASING OBESITY

If there is one health trend of the past thirty years that everyone can agree upon, it is the increasing prevalence of obesity in all segments of our population. In a study published in 1995, the authors compared rates of obesity for black and white boys and girls between the NHANES study, done in 1963–1965, NHANES II, done in 1976–1980, and NHANES III, done in 1988–1991.[13] They defined obesity as a body mass index (BMI) above the 95th percentile for age and sex. In the 1963–1965 study, about 5 percent of children had a BMI greater than the 95th percentile, which is what one would expect. However, by 1988–1991, the percentage of obese 6-to-11-year-olds had increased markedly, as shown in Table 4. I

TABLE 4: PERCENTAGE OF 6-TO-11-YEAR-OLD CHILDREN WITH A BMI GREATER THAN
THE 95TH PERCENTILE BASED ON FOUR NATIONAL SURVEYS SPANNING FIVE DECADES

Years of study	White boys	Black boys	White girls	Black girls
1963–1965	5.6	2.0	5.1	5.3
1976–1980	7.9	7.9	6.4	11.3
1988–1991	10.4	13.4	10.2	16.2
1999–2000	12.0	17.1	11.6	22.2

have added to the table the recently published results of
NHANES 1999–2000.[14] Note that the greatest increase was
found in black girls, in which a stunning 22 percent were
found to be obese before they even reached adolescence.
Black males lag behind the females, but their rates of obesity
are very sobering as well. Similar increases were noted in 12-
to-17-year-olds. Numerous studies have confirmed these
trends, which are taking place in both sexes, at all ages, and in
all racial and ethnic groups. A big reason that linking early
puberty to obesity makes so much sense is that, unlike environmental exposures, which tend to affect some geographic
areas much more than others, obesity is widespread and
prevalent throughout the United States. It is hard to deny that
exposure of our young children to obesity has been a nationwide trend of sufficient magnitude to potentially have im-
pacted on reproductive processes.

It doesn't take a great deal of thought to come up with a
list of factors that have contributed to this worrisome picture. The increase in caloric intake during the past twenty to
thirty years can be related to an increase in intake of foods
high in fat and sugar, including fast foods, which even fami-

lies in the lower socioeconomic categories may consume two or more times a week. School lunches are notorious for their high fat content, and vending machines dispensing soda containing 180–210 calories per can are present in most schools above the elementary level. Even meals eaten at home are more likely to include prepackaged or processed foods richer in fat and calories. The availability of low-fat and fat-free alternatives has not made a dent in the number of calories the average American consumes. Add to this the dramatic decrease in physical activity of American children. After school, leisure time is much more likely to be spent in front of a TV or computer screen or with a handheld video game than outside in the yard or on a playground. Many schools have cut back on their physical education programs. And as a society, we are walking far less than we used to and driving to most places that could be reached by walking a mile or less.

So what does the trend toward increasing obesity have to do with the earlier age of puberty in girls? It has long been known that overweight girls tend to mature earlier than girls of normal weight, and that thin girls tend to mature later. Although there does not seem to be a critical level of fatness that triggers menarche, as Dr. Rose Frisch proposed in the early 1970s, this relationship has been observed in enough studies that there must be some logical connection. The question that occurred to me as I became more involved in the puberty story was: Could I find evidence that the earlier onset of puberty over the past twenty to thirty years was related to increasing obesity? The idea of using the PROS data was attractive, since the data were already collected, saving a great deal of time and effort. It contained information on a population of girls of varying degrees of fatness or thinness whose pubertal stage was known. As I was mulling this over, I was contacted in early 1998 by one of the authors of the PROS study asking if I knew any endocrinologists who might be interested in helping with additional analyses of the data to examine the puberty-obesity connection. I quickly volunteered myself for the task and started a collaboration with Dr. Herman-Giddens, Eric Slora, the statistician for PROS, and Dr. Richard Wasserman of the University of Vermont, one of the senior authors of the PROS puberty study.

Since height and weight were measured on each girl, we could easily calculate the body mass index (BMI = weight [in kilograms]/height [in meters]^2), which is a widely used index of obesity and correlates fairly well with the percentage of body fat.[15] We then needed to locate "normal" data on BMI of contemporary 6-to-9-year-old girls (mean ± standard deviation), which had been recently published based on the NHANES III study.[16] The next step was to compare each girl's BMI with what was normal for her age by calculating what we called the BMI standard deviation score, or z score. This is a statistical measure that is equal to 0 if the girl's BMI is average for her age, positive if it is above average, and negative if it is below average. Then we could test the hypothesis that the 6-to-9-year-old girls who had already started breast development at an earlier age than average were more obese than the girls of the same age and race who had not. Over the next two years, Eric Slora did the statistical analyses I requested, and I mulled them over and discussed them with Drs. Herman-Giddens and Wasserman; our paper was finally published in *Pediatrics* in August 2001.[17]

The key findings of the study were that the 6-to-9-year-old girls with early breast development had significantly higher BMI z scores than the girls of the same age and race who were prepubertal, but to our surprise, this difference was more impressive for white girls than black girls (see Figures 5 and 6). One of my hypotheses was that black girls matured a year earlier than white girls because they had a tendency to be more overweight. However, when we factored in the difference in BMI Z scores between black and white girls, black girls still had an earlier onset of puberty than white girls. Another interesting finding related to pubic hair. We knew that appearance of pubic hair was also earlier according to the PROS and NHANES III studies than it had

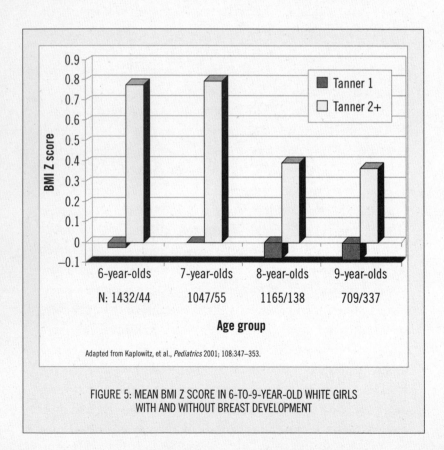

Adapted from Kaplowitz, et al., *Pediatrics* 2001; 108:347–353.

FIGURE 5: MEAN BMI Z SCORE IN 6-TO-9-YEAR-OLD WHITE GIRLS
WITH AND WITHOUT BREAST DEVELOPMENT

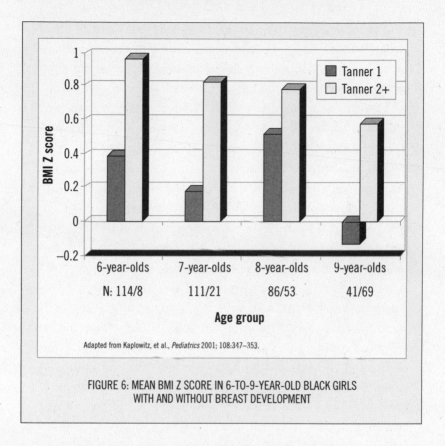

Adapted from Kaplowitz, et al., *Pediatrics* 2001; 108:347–353.

FIGURE 6: MEAN BMI Z SCORE IN 6-TO-9-YEAR-OLD BLACK GIRLS
WITH AND WITHOUT BREAST DEVELOPMENT

been twenty or thirty years ago. When we looked at 6-to-9-year-old black and white girls who had pubic hair but no breasts (these are basically girls with premature adrenarche, as defined in chapter 2), they were also more overweight than girls of the same age and race who were prepubertal. Thus, being more overweight seems to increase the risk of a girl having earlier pubic hair as well as early breast development, even though the hormonal regulation of the two events is quite different, as I pointed out in chapter 1. Other researchers have reported that girls with premature adrenarche tend to be more resistant to the actions of insulin than other girls, and since insulin resistance is one of the consequences of obesity, one can see how obesity and early pubic hair development might be linked.

One of the problems with a cross-sectional study such as the PROS study is that it can examine a large number of subjects, but each at only one point in time. Therefore, it can establish associations but not cause and effect. In this case, the question we would like to answer but cannot with certainty is this: Is the increased obesity we are seeing the *cause* of the trend for earlier puberty, as I propose, or is the earlier puberty causing the obesity due, as many people in the field believe, to an effect of increasing estrogens on storage of body fat? It is known that as puberty progresses in females, estrogen levels and body fat content rise in parallel, and it is known that in adult women, estrogens and progesterone from the ovaries favor the storage of excess calories as fat, explaining the major difference in adult body fat composition between men and women. My argument is that when we look at girls who are at the earliest stages of puberty, the estrogen levels are only minimally elevated, and I do not believe that there has been sufficient estrogen exposure to cause the increased obesity we are seeing. Rather, I would argue, it is the pre-existing obesity in 6-to-9-year-old girls that is one of the main reasons that they start maturing so early. Support for my view comes from two recent studies. In one study involving 319 Swedish schoolgirls, a greater change in BMI between ages 2 and 8 (i.e., a greater increase in fatness) predicted an earlier timing of the pubertal growth spurt by 0.7 years compared to girls with a lesser increase in BMI.[18] In the second study, fatness measured at age 5 before any signs of puberty were evident was a predictor of a greater likelihood of having breast development at age 7 or 9.[19] Although these findings are quite consistent with the hypothesis that fat causes early puberty, some might still argue that the issue has not been completely settled.

So why does it make sense that increased fat would lead to earlier puberty in girls? Over the past ten years, evidence has accumulated that leptin, a protein made by fat cells that is known to control appetite and body composition, also is involved in the regulation of puberty.[20] In mice that are unable to produce leptin, gonadotropin levels are low and puberty does not occur unless the missing leptin is replaced. In rare humans who have been discovered with either the inability to make or respond to leptin, gonadotropins are also low and there is no progression through puberty. Studies of normal girls show that leptin levels rise progressively during puberty, starting at 7–8 years, well before the rise in LH and estradiol, suggesting that rising leptin could be a trigger for the production of the puberty hormones.[21,22,23] In boys, the situation is different. The same studies showed that as puberty progresses, unlike the situation in girls, leptin levels fall by age 13 to levels only about one-third of those found in females. This seems to relate in part to the fact that fat mass increases during puberty in girls, while in boys, under the influence of testosterone, muscle mass increases but not fat mass. If a critical level of leptin were needed for puberty to start and progress, this would certainly explain why fatter girls, who have higher leptin levels (blood leptin is directly related to fat cell mass), mature earlier and thin girls mature later. This also makes a great deal of sense evolutionarily, since adequate stores of fat are needed to ensure a healthy pregnancy. In our human ancestors, who likely at times had limited food supplies (for example, if there was a drought), there would be no point in a young woman being able to get pregnant if she did not have enough fat stores to carry a pregnancy to term.

A Hypothesis as to Why There Is No Apparent Trend for Earlier Puberty in Boys

At this point, I would like to bring into the discussion boys, whom I have neglected for almost this entire book. As I mentioned earlier, there are no clear data indicating that boys are entering puberty earlier now than they were twenty or thirty years ago (there appears to be a trend detected in the NHANES III study for earlier pubic hair, but that likely reflects an earlier increase in adrenal androgens).[24] My colleagues and I still see relatively few boys for evaluation of early puberty, and most of those we do see have premature adrenarche, not true precocious puberty. Why the difference between girls and boys in this respect? The reason, I believe, is that, unlike in girls, increased body fat does not usually lead to earlier puberty in boys. Although data on this subject are sparse, a study from Italy published in 1988 showed that while obese girls, as expected, had earlier puberty and menses, obesity was not associated with early puberty in boys; in fact, about 20 percent of obese boys had delayed puberty.[25] A study published in 2002 based on the NHANES III data showed that while girls with earlier-than-average puberty were more likely to be overweight than those not undergoing early puberty, boys with early puberty were less likely to be overweight (i.e., they were thinner) than those not experiencing early puberty.[26] In my own clinic, I have seen about twelve boys over the years with delayed puberty who were obese but had nothing else wrong with them, leading me to suspect that in some boys obesity could contribute not to early puberty but to a delay in it.

My reasoning as to why this makes sense is as follows: Once a male impregnates a female, his contribution to maintaining the pregnancy is over. Early in the evolution of our species, there was no advantage in terms of survival of the fetus for males to have increased fat stores. Therefore, there was no evolutionary pressure in males to link the onset and progression of puberty to greater fat stores and higher leptin levels, as there was in females. Unlike in females, leptin levels in males actually decrease during puberty. Thus being overweight might even have the effect of slowing puberty by raising leptin levels and thus counteracting the natural fall in leptin as boys progress through puberty.

So Why Do Black Girls Start to Mature a Year Earlier than White Girls?

Three large studies done in the late 1980s and early 1990s, the PROS study and NHANES III (which have already been discussed), and the National Heart, Lung, and Blood Institute Growth and Health Study,[27] show clearly that black girls started developing breasts and pubic hair about a year earlier than white girls and started their menses about a half year earlier. The question is what factors might explain this difference. One possibility, that it is a consequence of the greater degree of obesity in black girls, was not supported by the analysis done on the PROS data. One could hypothesize that there is something in the environment in which black children grow up that causes them to mature earlier, but it is difficult to point to a plausible environmental factor. The possible effect of living in single-parent homes needs to be investigated further, but in my own practice, most of the early-maturing black girls I have seen are living with both parents. The living standard of black children is on the average somewhat lower than that of white children, but the PROS study found no evidence that whether or not a girl was covered by Medicaid (an indicator of low socioeconomic status) was predictive of earlier puberty. Another possibility is that decreased physical activity in black children might somehow be involved. However, the evidence at present points more to the possibility that genes that are more common within the black population than the white population are somehow responsible.

What genes might be responsible? There is now abundant evidence from studies in adults and teenagers that sensitivity to insulin is lower in black than in white subjects. These studies involve careful measurement of blood insulin levels when the blood glucose is experimentally held constant, and the results could simply reflect greater obesity of the black subjects. However, studies done by Dr. Silva Arslanian and her colleagues at the Children's Hospital in Pittsburgh show that even in children who have not started puberty, in which the differences in BMI between black and white children were minimal, the racial difference in insulin sensitivity was readily apparent.[28] A genetic difference in insulin sensitivity is thought to explain why type 2 diabetes, in which insulin resistance plays a key role, is much more common in black adults and children than in whites. As noted above, insulin resistance is often seen in girls with premature adrenarche, which could explain why premature adrenarche is more common in blacks and why pubic hair growth starts a year earlier. The possibility that insulin resistance is part of the underlying process that can lead to precocious puberty in girls is something which clearly requires further investigation. Another study that may shed light on the racial difference in the timing of puberty involved measurement of leptin in the blood in seventy-nine white and fifty-seven black 8-to-17-year-old girls in Houston. Not surprisingly, black girls had leptin levels that were on average nearly 80 percent higher than those in white girls, which could reflect the 32 percent greater amount of body fat. However, even after correcting for body fat, leptin levels were still higher in the black girls.[29] Thus, one can postulate a genetic difference in leptin production in black girls, leading to higher leptin levels in prepubertal children and thus a tendency to start puberty at earlier ages.

CHAPTER 6

GETTING THE MOST
FROM A VISIT TO A
PEDIATRIC ENDOCRINOLOGIST

S o let us say that you have a child who has some of the signs of early puberty, and your primary-care physician has suggested the child be seen by a specialist. This chapter will discuss what you can do to make the experience most helpful to you and least traumatic for the child.

FINDING A SPECIALIST
TO HELP EVALUATE THE PROBLEM

Anyone who is trained as a pediatric endocrinologist should have experience in this area, since it is one of the most common problems we are asked to see. Most medium-to-large cities will have at least one such specialist, usually affiliated with a teaching hospital, though in the larger cities, some specialists are in private practice and not affiliated with a teaching hospital or university. The child's primary-care physician will usually recommend a specialist to whom he or she has referred children with similar problems in the past. If you live in a town that has adult endocrinologists but no pediatric endocrinologists, it may be worth the extra travel, even if it means a drive of three or four hours, to see a pediatric specialist who has more experience with puberty issues. One way to find the specialist closest to you is to look on the Web site of the Lawson Wilkins Pediatric Endocrine Society, at www.lwpes.org. The majority of practicing pediatric endocrinologists belong to this society, though it takes at least two years after completion of a pediatric endocrine fellowship to be able to join.

As in any field of medicine, specialists in the field of pediatric endocrinology differ in how they approach certain problems, and this is particularly true of early puberty in girls. If you have a choice of several specialists, it is difficult to know ahead of time which one will have an approach with which you will feel the most comfortable. There are those of us who tend to be more conservative, rely more on our clinical judgment, do fewer tests, and are less likely to treat a girl who is borderline in terms of her age of developing signs of puberty. Others are more aggressive, more likely to run a large battery of tests, and more likely to treat borderline cases with medication. If you have a definite preference for one style or the other, the primary-care physician may be able to suggest a specialist who will best meet your needs, but in many cases, you will simply have to accept whomever they recommend, and hope for the best.

WHAT KINDS OF INFORMATION WILL THE PEDIATRIC ENDOCRINOLOGIST NEED TO EVALUATE THE PROBLEM?

A family history is a good place to start. The timing of puberty has a strong genetic component, and many children with signs of early puberty have a parent or a close relative on either side of the family who also had signs of early puberty. The importance of this is that if there is a clear genetic predisposition, it means that your child is less likely to have a serious underlying problem causing early puberty. At a minimum, you should be prepared to tell the specialist the age at which the child's mother started breast development and the age at which her menses started. If the child's problem is mainly pubic hair development, it would be helpful to know when the mother first developed pubic hair, though this is less likely to be recalled than the age of menarche. It is also helpful to know if the father was an early maturer relative to his peers. Boys who start puberty at the average age of 11 or 12 usually have their growth spurt between ages 13 and 14 and have largely completed their growth by 16 or 17, so a growth spurt prior to age 13 should be considered early. If the father started shaving regularly before his peers, that would also suggest somewhat early puberty. Information about the timing of puberty and menses in sisters or brothers or even half siblings is also useful, especially if they are older than the child in question. While it may not be necessary to get exhaustive information on other relatives, it is worth checking to see if any aunts, uncles, cousins, or grandparents are known to have had early onset of puberty. Of all of the above, the most reliable information you will have is the age of menarche in female relatives of the child. I have found that mothers have a hard time remembering when their breast development started, presumably because it happened gradually and did not have the emotional impact of their first period. I have had several mothers insist that their breast development started around the same time or even after they began having periods, which seems unlikely given that at least two years of exposure to pubertal levels of estrogens is needed to prepare the uterus for menstrual periods.

Before the visit, it is helpful to try to remember when the child began having either breast development, pubic hair growth, or both. In some cases, this is impossible to say, because the problem was noted by the child's primary-care physician on a well-child exam, and neither the parent nor the child had noticed it before. However, if one can tell the specialist that the breast tissue or pubic hair has been there for six months or twelve months, this is very useful information. If the breasts are still of modest size (stage 2 on the Tanner scale), or there is still only a small amount of pubic hair, the likelihood is that whatever is happening is not progressing very rapidly. If I am told that the small amount of breast tissue or pubic hair that I find on the first visit has changed little over the past six or more months, this decreases significantly the chances that we are dealing with true precocious puberty, where progression over a six-month period is the rule, not the exception.

By far the most useful information that can be provided at the time of the initial visit is a growth chart, or at least a list of heights and weights covering the past two to three years. The reason is that growth acceleration is one of the major clues we look for to tell us whether a young girl with some breast development may actually be progressing through puberty. If all we know is that at the initial visit the child's height is at the 95th percentile, that may suggest rapid growth, but what if she was also at the 95th percentile two years ago? In that case, the rate of growth may still be normal (2–2½ inches per year), and the child might just be a tall child who has not yet truly started puberty. On the other hand, if two years ago her height was at the 75th percentile and she is now at the

95th percentile, the chances that she is already having a pubertal growth spurt are good, and this would weigh heavily in my decision as to how much testing to do and whether or not to order a bone age test.

If the child has been seeing the same primary-care physician for the last two or three years, that office should have in the child's file a plotted growth chart, which should be faxed or mailed to the specialist to whom the child has been referred. I have my staff request this routinely whenever a child with a puberty problem is referred, but it is disheartening how often this critical information fails to materialize by the time of the visit. Sometimes the referring physician's office intends to send it but doesn't get around to it. On a few occasions, the material has been faxed but never quite makes it into the child's chart. Sometimes the child is being seen in the referring physician's practice for the first time, and the office has no previous growth data. Or a child who is 8 years old may not have had a well-child visit since she started kindergarten three years earlier. In most offices, height and weight are not done when the child comes in for a sick visit, and once a child starts school, the regularity of well-child visits decreases significantly.

I believe it is the responsibility of the parent to make sure that any relevant growth data that exist on the young girl are brought to the appointment. One way to make sure this happens is to go by the primary-care physician's office and have them make a copy of the growth chart to bring to the visit. They may say they have sent it already, but it is better for the specialists to have two copies of the growth chart than none. If there is no growth chart in the child's file (this happens more often in the offices of family practitioners than pediatricians), at least have them write down any recorded heights and weights for the past three years. If the child is 7 or 8, the separate growth chart for the first three years of life (which is usually more complete because children are being seen regularly for immunizations and well-child exams) is less useful than the growth chart that covers the period from age 2 years on, but if that is all that's available, bring it. (For a 1-to-3-year-old the 0–3 growth chart will have all the necessary measurements.) If the child was being seen until recently by another physician in the same area or has moved from out of state, it may be that the child's growth chart was sent to her new primary-care physician, but more often than not this is not requested, and even if it was requested, it is not always done. In this case, the parent needs to contact the previous physician and request that the growth records be sent *directly to the parent* (not to the new physician, if they are needed quickly). Since most offices have a policy of requiring that the request for records be submitted in writing, you should not put this off until a few days before the child's appointment. If it has been put off until the last minute, faxing a request and having the records faxed to you may work, though copies of records are usually easier to read than faxes.

There are sources of useful growth information other than physician records that should not be overlooked. In some states, though in fewer than in the past, schools measure children once or twice a year. These measurements tend to be done in a hurry, frequently with shoes on, so their accuracy is not as great as those done in a physician's office, but they are often sufficient to establish a baseline growth pattern and make it possible to detect a recent acceleration of growth. Also, do not neglect measurements that may have been done at home, using pencil marks or a chart taped to a wall or door. Again, if there are enough of these, the specialist can use them to supplement other growth measurements to establish the previous growth pattern and see if there has been a recent change.

Is It Helpful to Have Lab Tests and X Rays Done Prior to the Visit?

I will discuss in detail in chapter 7 the specific lab tests and X rays that might be helpful in the evaluation of early puberty. The question here is whether or not it is a good idea to have them ordered by the primary-care physician prior to the visit with the pediatric endocrinologist. I can think of only a few occasions when having test results for a girl with possible precocious puberty at the time of the initial visit made my task easier. Far more often, I find that tests were done that I would not have ordered; less often, tests that would really have been helpful were not done. If the primary-care physician calls me to discuss the case, I may request that specific tests be done ahead of time. However, in the majority of girls I have seen with signs of early puberty, particularly in girls with premature adrenarche and premature thelarche, I am able to make the diagnosis with no tests or X rays at all. In those cases, having to explain to parents the meaning of possibly abnormal results of tests that I would not have ordered in the first place is a distraction. (The most common situation of this sort is mildly elevated estrogen levels, a very common problem even in girls with no breast development, as I will discuss in the next chapter.)

If the primary-care physician has ordered a bone age test, most specialists in my field like to read the X ray themselves, rather than just rely on the report of a radiologist. Therefore, it is suggested that a copy of the X ray be obtained and brought to the initial visit. However, I find bone age X rays helpful only some of the time and would prefer that I make the decision as to whether to order one. Overall, my advice would be to wait until the appointment to see what tests, if any, the specialist will want done. My experience is that most primary-care physicians will want a specialist to see a girl who has early breasts or pubic hair growth, regardless of what the test results or X rays show, so doing the tests ahead of time is unlikely to make the visit unnecessary. Therefore, if the question of testing comes up when the referral is discussed, it is very appropriate to say, "Why don't we wait and see what tests the specialist wants to order? That way we can make sure our child only has to go through it once."

How to Prepare the Child for Her Visit to a Pediatric Endocrinologist

The amount of anxiety a visit to a pediatric specialist will generate varies tremendously from child to child. Many girls I have seen are not the slightest bit concerned about their breast or pubic hair development and have no problem permitting the physician to do a complete physical exam. Only a minority come in very upset either about the prospect of having their "privates" examined or having blood drawn. In a few cases, parents have called me ahead of time wanting to find out exactly what I was going to do so that they could prepare their child. This is quite difficult to do over the phone, since my approach will depend a lot on what I find when I review the growth chart and examine the child. What follows is a list of points I would go over with the child ahead of time, realizing that every child is different and some will want to know a lot more than others about what to expect. I think this list will cover most of the situations that may be encountered, and will likely reassure more than alarm.

- "Dr. _____ noticed [or agreed with us] during your last visit that you were starting to develop breasts [or have hair around your vagina] at an earlier age than most girls do. Often this is a very minor problem and does not require any treatment, but to be sure, he wants you to be seen by a specialist."
- "Dr. _____, whom your doctor suggested we see, has special training in the area of early puberty in girls. She will want to know how you feel about the changes that are happening to your body, so please tell her if you feel upset about starting to mature so early or if anyone has teased you about your body."
- "The doctor will want to measure you carefully and see how you compare with other children your age on a growth chart. When the doctor examines you I will be with you the whole time. It will be like what your regular doctor does, except that more attention will be paid to two special parts of your body: your breasts, which she will want to look at carefully and perhaps measure with a ruler, and your vagina, to see if you have started to grow hair around it and how much of it there is. The doctor may need to gently spread apart the outer part of your vagina to get a better look, but it will not be necessary to put a finger or anything else inside it. If you are frightened or don't understand what the doctor is doing, please ask her and I'm sure it will be explained."

- If you are going to see a pediatric endocrinologist at a teaching hospital, you should be prepared for the possibility that he or she will be working with a medical student or a doctor who is training to be a pediatrician. Most young girls are fine with having one or two other doctors besides the specialist examine them, but the child can be told that if having several people examining her makes her uncomfortable, she should tell the doctor.

- "I can't tell you if you will need any blood tests, since the doctor won't decide until after she has talked to us, examined you, and looked at your growth chart. If you do need tests, I am sure that they have people to do it who are very good at working with children."

- "It is possible you will need an X ray, but if you do, you will probably only have to put your hand on a flat box that has film in it while a technician takes a picture of your hand, so the doctor can see how fast your bones are maturing."

- "After the doctor has talked to us, done her exam, and gotten the results of any tests she ordered, we will be told whether anything more needs to be done. Most of the time, developing early is something that can just be watched and doesn't need treatment, but we just want to be sure it isn't anything more serious."

SUGGESTIONS FOR THE VISIT

I believe there are two keys to a successful visit to any specialist. First, the specialist should be able to explain what he or she thinks about the problem he or she is being asked to consult on concisely and in language that is clear to someone without any medical background. Second, the specialist should allow ample time for questions and make sure that the patient and family do not feel rushed. The amount of time you are with the specialist is not critical, as long as those two conditions are met. As readers of this book, you are way ahead of most families in this situation in that you will know the major possibilities the specialist will need to consider, what information you will be asked to give, what he or she will be looking for on the exam, and what tests, if any, will need to be done. Most people in my field are quite good at giving explanations in a family-friendly way, but if you are having trouble following what you are being told, don't be shy. Make clear what points you are having trouble with and request whatever additional information you need to help you understand what is going on. Don't worry that your questions might be dumb or that the doctor will be upset if you ask too many. I personally prefer working with families who take an active role in trying to understand what is going on, as opposed to those who sit there passively while I speak.

If the specialist wants to order tests, you have every right to ask what they are and what helpful information they will provide. You should also get an estimate of how long it will take for the results to come back; make sure you have given a phone number where you can be reached during the day. You should also leave the office with a clear idea of what the follow-up plan will be. In some cases, when I am convinced the diagnosis is premature adrenarche or premature thelarche, I will order no tests and schedule no follow-up, but I will always send a letter to the referring physician explaining why I am not concerned. However, I will add a comment about what the physician might look for at future visits that might concern me and make me want to see the child again. In other cases, I might want to see the child back in four to six months to see if any of the signs of puberty have progressed or not. If I have ordered lab tests, I will often not decide how soon to see the child again until I have reviewed the test results. In most hospitals, some of the special tests we will discuss in the next chapter are sent to outside laboratories, but usually the results are back within five to seven days. Allowing for a few extra days and a weekend, you should expect to hear about the test results within two weeks, and if you have not, you should not hesitate to call and leave a message for the specialist to call you back.

———

In summary, a visit to a pediatric endocrinologist is commonly suggested when a young girl develops any signs of early puberty, and it does not mean that the child has a serious problem. The visit can be most productive (1) if the parent makes sure the specialist has the family history and growth information he or she needs ahead of time or brings it to the visit, (2) if the child is told in a straightforward way what to expect before the visit, and (3) if the parent makes sure that all his or her questions are addressed during the visit, including the follow-up plan.

CHAPTER 7

A WORRIED PARENT'S GUIDE TO LAB TESTS COMMONLY USED TO EVALUATE EARLY PUBERTY

A common source of anxiety for parents who are having their children evaluated for early puberty is that specialists may order a lot of blood tests and X rays but often do not take adequate time to explain the purpose of the tests or the meaning of the results when they come back. This chapter will attempt to take the mystery out of the tests that are often done and explain how they may or may not help pin down the cause of early puberty in young girls. I need to make clear my own bias at the beginning, however. I believe that in over half of the young girls referred to specialists with signs of early puberty, the diagnosis is sufficiently clear from the history and the exam so that no tests whatsoever are necessary. If tests are done "just to be sure" and the results are not exactly what the physician was expecting, it often results in doing further tests, which in my experience usually clouds an otherwise clear picture and causes needless concern on the part of the parents. Another common problem with tests, particularly when they are ordered by the primary-care physician, is that the wrong tests are ordered for the child's specific signs of puberty, and both time and money are wasted. The most common example of this is the young girl whose only sign of puberty is pubic hair, but the primary-care physician orders tests for LH, FSH, and estradiol. These tests may be helpful in disclosing the cause of early breast development but have nothing at all to do with pubic hair. As mentioned earlier, pubic hair growth is due to adrenal androgens, not estrogens, which are not regulated by the pituitary hormones LH and FSH.

I will start by discussing the specific hormone tests that are frequently ordered to evaluate early puberty. For further information on the actions of the specific hormones, please refer back to chapter 1.

GONADOTROPINS: LH AND FSH

In theory, a single measurement of LH and FSH, the pituitary hormones that stimulate the ovaries, should be the most reliable tests to help a pediatric endocrinologist decide if a young girl has actually started puberty. In practice, it is not so simple. The reason is that with the most widely used method for measuring LH and FSH in the blood (by radioimmunoassay or RIA), there is a large overlap between what is measured in girls who are prepubertal and those who are in early puberty. Part of the explanation is that because the hypothalamic-releasing factor GnRH is secreted in a pulsatile manner, levels of LH and FSH rise and fall about every two hours. Also, some researchers believe that LH and FSH levels measured by the RIA method do not accurately reflect the true activity of these hormones in prepubertal children. More accurate results are obtained with a relatively new method for measuring LH and FSH in the blood called the immunochemiluminometric assay, but only some labs use this procedure.

One confusing aspect of interpreting LH and FSH results is that although both hormones rise as puberty progresses, the LH test is a far more reliable indicator of puberty than the FSH test. For example, girls with premature thelarche often have an LH level so low that it is undetectable but an FSH level that is much higher. Thus levels of FSH are by themselves of little use in deciding whether a young girl is in puberty.

The GnRH Stimulation Test

One way to get around the difficulty of interpreting single LH and FSH levels is to obtain a baseline blood sample and then to give an injection into a vein of GnRH and obtain further blood samples up to sixty minutes later, when the medication will have had a chance to stimulate the pituitary to release both LH and FSH. It was shown back in the 1970s that how much LH and FSH are released after injecting GnRH is closely related to the stage of puberty. The underlying explanation is that once puberty has started and the gonadotropin-producing cells in the pituitary (gonadotropes) have been exposed chronically to pulses of GnRH, their ability to release LH in response to a sudden increase in GnRH is enhanced. Several studies have shown that one can get reliable information from the GnRH test by obtaining a single sample thirty to forty-five minutes after injecting GnRH, but many physicians still obtain samples at zero, fifteen, thirty, forty-five, and sixty minutes, which is a lot more expensive but gives no more information than a single sample does. In Table 5, I have given an example of how the GnRH test might look in two young girls. In a prepubertal child (or in a child with premature thelarche or adrenarche), both the unstimulated LH level and the increase in LH after GnRH are small, while the increase in FSH (for unknown reasons) tends to be much greater. Once the child has definitely started puberty, even if she is still early in puberty, the randomly obtained LH level before GnRH may not have increased much, but the LH response to GnRH is now usually greater than the FSH response (or "LH-predominant"). For many years, the gold standard for determining if a young child with some physical changes of puberty had actually started puberty was that the response had to be LH-predominant and the LH level after GnRH had to be over 15–20. With the newer immunochemiluminometric assay, which gives lower numbers, some researchers have said that the LH needs to rise only to 8 for the result to be considered pubertal. Many physicians are no longer even measuring FSH, making it hard to tell if the response to GnRH is LH-predominant or not.

If the above section has confused you, it is understandable, because I think a lot of physicians who do GnRH test-

TABLE 5: TYPICAL RESULTS FOR GNRH TESTING IN PREPUBERTAL
AND PUBERTAL GIRLS (IN MILLIUNITS PER ML BY RIA METHOD)

	Prepubertal girl		Pubertal girl	
	Before GnRH	After GnRH	Before GnRH	After GnRH
LH	0.1	5	1.5	26
FSH	3.0	20	2.3	12

ing are confused as well. Over the years, I have had the chance to either take over the care of or give a second opinion on many girls who had been given a GnRH test by another physician. I have seen many cases where another specialist in my field interpreted a test as showing that a young girl was in puberty and used that result to justify treatment, when I would have interpreted the same results as indicating the child was *not* in puberty. This most often occurred when the increase in FSH after GnRH was large (sometimes to greater than 30) but the increase in LH was much smaller (an FSH-predominant response). FSH-predominant responses, sometimes with quite high FSH levels, are the rule in premature thelarche. Yet some physicians ignore or overlook this and view *any* large increase in LH *or* FSH as a sign that the gonadotropes are revved up and ready to start producing enough LH and FSH to cause the child to progress through puberty.

My view is that when a girl has her initial evaluation for early breast development, it is not unreasonable to order a single LH and FSH test, even though they do not always give clear results, but the GnRH test should be used sparingly. In most situations, the child has to return on a separate day for the test (since the GnRH usually has to be ordered specially) and either an IV needs to be started or the child has to be stuck at least two separate times. The form of GnRH used for this test is expensive, and for the past two years it has been in very short supply around the country. The test is rarely necessary in girls who start breasts before age 3 (unless the progression is rapid), since they nearly always have premature thelarche. For older girls who have a small amount of breast development, one will likely learn more by having her reexamined by the same physician in four to six months than by doing a GnRH test. One can be fairly certain that 8-year-old girls who have growth acceleration and progressive breast development are in puberty, and so doing a GnRH test will not add much to the evaluation. In my opinion, the test is most useful in 3-to-7-year-old girls who have enough breast enlargement that they may be in early puberty, so treatment has been considered. However, one wants to be sure the diagnosis is truly central precocious puberty before undertaking treatment, which will be discussed in chapter 8. In rare cases, both the LH and the FSH are low before GnRH, and neither one rises after GnRH; the diagnosis in that case is some form of peripheral precocious puberty, and one would need to consider either an ovarian tumor or cyst or McCune-Albright syndrome. In these cases, other diagnostic tests need to be done (for example, an ultrasound of the ovaries), and the usual treatment for true or central precocious puberty will be ineffective.

ESTRADIOL

This test is also one that is helpful in theory but less helpful in practice. A girl who has started puberty should have a mildly elevated estradiol for her age, since after all it is estradiol alone that causes progressive breast enlargement. However, studies have shown that in some girls who are clearly pubertal by their physical exam, the estradiol level in the blood may be too low to measure (in such cases, LH and FSH will be pubertal and there will be an LH-predominant response to GnRH). More often in my experience, girls who are definitely *not* in puberty (e.g., they may have pubic hair but little or no breast tissue) may have estradiol levels in the range that suggests they *have* started puberty. One should therefore be very careful in using the blood level of estradiol to make decisions regarding treatment. I have seen several cases in which endocrinologists have treated girls for precocious puberty who had little or no breast tissue and no increase in growth rate, solely because the estradiol was slightly elevated. In such cases, estradiol may remain elevated even after treatment, which may lead the physician to try increasing the dose of the medication to suppress puberty, though it really isn't true precocious puberty at all. If a young girl has signs of progressive puberty and LH and FSH are in the pubertal range, *then* a pubertal level of estradiol is helpful. I try to avoid the problem of trying to explain away a falsely elevated estradiol level by not even ordering the test unless I am very concerned about the possibility of true precocious puberty. Unfortunately, the test is often ordered by the referring physician before I even see the child, and then I have to explain to the parent why this particular test cannot be trusted. On very rare occasions, one may find a very high estradiol and very low LH and FSH; if there is rapid progression of breast development, this would raise concerns about an ovarian tumor or a large estrogen-producing ovarian cyst. I have seen only two cases like that in my twenty years of practice. My advice is to be very skeptical of any treatment decision based mainly on whatever the estradiol level happens to be.

ADRENAL HORMONES (DHEA-S AND 17-HYDROXYPROGESTERONE)

When the main sign of puberty in a young girl is pubic hair, the most appropriate test to order, if one wants to order a test, is the DHEA-S. As mentioned in chapter 1, this is a storage form of the adrenal androgen DHEA, and it is nearly always present in young children with pubic or underarm hair and body odor. Typically, the result in a 3-to-8-year-old with pubic hair shows that DHEA-S is high for the age of the child but normal for an older child with the same amount of pubic hair. I used to order this test whenever I saw a child I felt had premature adrenarche, but I no longer do so, because the test result will only confirm what is obvious from the history and exam, namely, that the child is producing adrenal androgens at an earlier age than usual. The time when this test is necessary, in my opinion, is if the child has other signs of excessive androgen production, such as an enlarged clitoris (very rare), acne (uncommon), or rapid growth (not that unusual). A very high level of DHEA-S can be a sign of an androgen-producing adrenal tumor, which might lead the physician to order a CT scan or an MRI of the adrenals. In my career, I have seen two girls with virilizing adrenal tumors, one of whom was 3 and had an enlarged clitoris and one of whom was 12 and had severe acne and a deepening voice.

The 17-hydroxyprogesterone (17-OHP) test is necessary to diagnose a relatively rare cause of early pubic hair, congenital adrenal hyperplasia (CAH). In its classic or severe form, it will cause a girl to have ambiguous genitalia at birth, since there is severe overproduction of adrenal androgens starting during fetal life, and noticeable enlargement of the clitoris. What may show up in a 3-to-7-year-old is the mild or nonclassical form of CAH, which may be difficult to distinguish from premature adrenarche based on the exam. Some physicians will order the 17-OHP test on any young child with pubic hair. In children with mild CAH, the 17-OHP is usually well above the normal range, and levels slightly above normal rarely have any significance. However, if one has a borderline or increased 17-OHP, the only way to exclude the possibility of mild CAH is to do what is called an ACTH stimulation test, to stimulate the adrenals to put out more hormones and hormone precursors. A blood sample is drawn as a baseline, synthetic ACTH is injected, and a second sample for cortisol (which normally increases a lot after ACTH) and 17-OHP is drawn thirty to sixty minutes later. If the child happens to be of Eastern European Jewish descent, the incidence of this relatively rare genetic condition is increased, so screening for CAH makes more sense. However, in the black population, which makes up most of the patients I see with early pubic hair, this condition seems to be quite rare. I do not advocate screening for CAH unless there is something other than just pubic or axillary hair and body odor, such as growth acceleration, acne, or enlargement of the clitoris. Interpreting the results is not always easy, and I suspect some children who have been diagnosed with this condition (which can be treated with hydrocortisone given two or three times a day) do not really have it and just have benign premature adrenarche.

THYROID TESTS

Many years ago, a few cases were described in which children with severely underactive thyroid glands that had gone undiagnosed for many years developed precocious puberty. The reason this was thought to occur was complex, but this situation is quite rare and I have never seen it in over twenty years. The reason I am unlikely to have missed this is that a child needs to have a very underactive thyroid for a long time for this to occur, and there should be other signs and symptoms of a thyroid problem. These would typically include several of the following: poor growth (as opposed to the usual rapid growth in girls who are in puberty), fatigue, a dull and puffy facial appearance, dry skin, constipation, and feeling cold a lot of the time. I bring all this up because many textbooks recommend thyroid tests be done anytime a patient is evaluated for early puberty. If the tests are done and are clearly normal, as is usually the case, there is no problem. However, problems in interpreting thyroid tests properly are common. The hormone TSH (thyroid-stimulating hormone) is made by the pituitary and increases when the thyroid gland is sick and having trouble making enough thyroid hormones. However, in a child, borderline elevated levels of TSH are fairly common and may not be a reliable indicator of an underactive thyroid or the need to start the child on thyroid hormones. More important, borderline abnormal thyroid levels are *not* a cause of precocious puberty. So parents should be skeptical if they are told that their daughter with possible precocious puberty also has an underactive thyroid and that the two conditions may be related. At a minimum, unless the thyroid tests are strikingly abnormal, they should be repeated at least once before a decision on thyroid hormone treatment is made.

BONE AGE

An X ray of the hand to assess the degree of skeletal maturation is another test that is done too often and easily misinterpreted. In a young girl with physical evidence of progressive puberty and growth acceleration, obtaining a bone age may be useful if it is advanced by two or more years relative to the child's chronological age. That finding seems to predict continued rapid advance of puberty and may also suggest the possibility of short adult stature, as described in chapter 3. However, determination of a bone age from a hand X ray is an inexact science, and even in perfectly normal children bone age is often advanced by as much as a year. Too often, I have seen children in whom the decision to treat with expensive medications to slow puberty has been made based on a bone age that is advanced by only a year or less. In addition, it is not rare to see the bone age advanced by at least two years in girls with premature adrenarche, particularly if they are tall for their age and growing somewhat rapidly, which occurs in 15 percent of the girls I have seen in the past few years. Some physicians feel the need to do *something* when the bone age is advanced, but drugs designed to suppress true precocious puberty are of no value when the only hormonal abnormality is increased adrenal androgen production. There are certainly cases where a girl with early puberty is evaluated shortly after puberty has started and there is not enough time for the bone age to have advanced by more than a year. However, in such cases, it is better to follow the child at four-to-six-month intervals to see if the breasts are increasing rapidly and growth is rapid. If this occurs, then repeating the bone age study six to twelve months after the initial X ray may show evidence of rapid advancement in bone age (e.g., twelve months in a six-month period), and then the case for further testing and possibly treatment is stronger. On the other hand, studies show that many girls with early puberty do not have rapid bone age advancement, presumably because they have a slowly progressive form of precocious puberty (discussed further in chapter 8), and these girls do not require treatment.

I am not suggesting that bone age studies are of no value in girls with signs of early puberty. I do believe that for the majority of patients where the growth chart and physical exam strongly suggest a diagnosis of premature thelarche or adrenarche, or the signs of puberty are still very early, doing a bone age right away is not necessary and the risk of missing an extremely advanced bone age is much less than the risk of overreacting to a mildly advanced bone age by ordering more tests.

PELVIC ULTRASOUND

One of the problems encountered in evaluating girls with early puberty is the difficulty of knowing if the ovaries are enlarged. In a boy, it is very easy to tell on a physical exam if the diagnosis is likely to be central precocious puberty, because the testes will be enlarged. In a girl, the size of the ovaries can best be determined by bouncing sound waves off the structures in the pelvis, creating a fuzzy image that a skilled radiologist can interpret. The test can tell not only if the ovaries are bigger than one would see in a prepubertal child, but also if there is a cyst as small as ½ inch across, and if the uterus is enlarged, which occurs after long-term exposure to estrogens. In a girl with true precocious puberty, the finding that both ovaries are enlarged supports that diagnosis. However, if the physical changes and hormone testing have established the diagnosis, there is really nothing gained by doing an ultrasound, since the finding of enlarged ovaries will not affect the treatment decisions. In a girl who appears to have premature thelarche, if one finds anything, it is likely to be a small cyst, which is nothing to worry about because small cysts are normal in young ovaries and disappear on their own. I recall a case in which a 2-year-old girl with a small amount of breast tissue had a pelvic ultrasound done in another city that showed such a cyst on the left ovary. My colleague saw the child and decided it was necessary to repeat the study six months later to make sure the cyst had not grown. The second time, the cyst on the left ovary was no longer seen, but there was a similar one on the right ovary. I recall this created much anxiety in the parents, who had to be reassured that small ovarian cysts in a 2-year-old were not a sign of any disease.

The situation where a pelvic ultrasound is really necessary is when hormonal tests show elevated levels of estradiol but low levels of LH and FSH both before and after GnRH in a girl with progressive breast enlargement. As mentioned at the end of the first section in this chapter, one would then need to worry about peripheral precocious puberty due to an ovarian tumor (usually benign but sometimes quite large), a large ovarian cyst, or McCune-Albright syndrome. In my career, I have seen one girl (a 9-year-old) with an ovarian tumor, which had grown to the size of a grapefruit by the time I saw her, and one girl with a large ovarian cyst, which had to be removed. For the common causes of early puberty, pelvic ultrasound studies are unnecessary. On the positive side, they involve no radiation exposure and no need for injection of dyes, as is the case for CT scans and MRIs, which will be discussed next.

BRAIN IMAGING STUDIES

We now enter one of the more controversial areas in the management of precocious puberty: When does a child need an MRI or CT scan of the head? Both of these tests allow physicians to literally look inside the skull and view images that are cross sections of the brain. As technology has gotten better and better, the size of abnormal brain areas, such as tumors, that can be detected has gotten smaller and smaller, and the resolution is now well under ½ inch. The CT scan first came into use in the late 1970s and is still very adequate for most purposes. It is less expensive than the MRI (about $1,000 compared to about $1,500), but it exposes the brain to a lot more radiation. Doing an MRI takes less time, so keeping an anxious young girl perfectly still is less of a problem, and it can pick up some subtle abnormalities that a CT scan might miss. Either one can be very scary for both the child and the parent. For very young girls who cannot be instructed to stay still for the few minutes it takes to do an MRI, it may be necessary to put the child under light anesthesia with medications administered through an IV. This is a safe procedure if a physician properly trained in this technique is present, but it becomes more difficult to schedule and much more expensive.

As I mentioned in chapter 2, it has long been known that the majority of girls with precocious puberty display nothing abnormal when the brain is imaged, and we refer to these girls as having idiopathic precocious puberty. Many physicians seeing such a child do not want to take even a small chance of missing a tumor, so they tend to do a CT or MRI on every girl with signs of puberty before age 8. The problem with this approach is that with puberty starting earlier than ever, there are a lot of perfectly healthy 7-year-olds out there who just happen to be at the early end of the spectrum of normal pubertal development. Do they all need expensive imaging studies so that the parents can be reassured they do not have a tumor? Or can the physician use his or her judgment and only do these studies when the risk of finding something abnormal is judged to be increased? The approach that I and many of my colleagues have used is to do brain imaging studies either when the onset of puberty is before 6 or 7 years of age or when there is some suggestion in the history or the exam of a central nervous system problem. The most obvious example would be headaches that are becoming more frequent and severe. Brain tumors, especially those that grow rapidly, may eventually press on pain-sensitive structures within the brain, or they may cause obstruction of the flow of cerebrospinal fluid, resulting in enlargement of the fluid-filled spaces within the brain called the ventricles, a condition referred to as hydrocephalus. Increased pressure within the brain can impair the cranial nerves, some of which control eye movement, resulting in crossed eyes and double vision. Loss of vision can occur because the pituitary gland is very close to where the two optic nerves come together, called the optic chiasma. Loss of peripheral vision is especially worrisome but is often not mentioned by children, since central vision may be spared. New onset of seizures or a change in the type or severity of seizures may be another clue to a disorder inside the brain. Few would argue that a girl with precocious puberty and any of the above problems needs an MRI, but on rare occasions the growth of a tumor in the area of the pituitary or hypothalamus is so slow that no signs or symptoms are noticed.

Until recently, there were no solid data about the risk of finding a tumor or something else abnormal on a brain MRI or CT in girls. (There was also not much data on boys, but the consensus is that the risk of a tumor is high enough that any boy with onset of central precocious puberty before age 9 needs brain imaging.) In January 2002, a group of doctors from Paris published an article in *Pediatrics* in which they described the findings of brain imaging studies in about two hundred girls with onset of breast development before age 8, all of whom had hormonal studies consistent with central precocious puberty.[1] One reason they collected and published their data was their concern that if the new puberty guidelines that I helped develop were followed, 7-year-old girls with precocious puberty due to brain tumors might be missed because their physicians would not refer them to a specialist for a full evaluation. They found that if the girl was younger than age 6, the chance of her having an abnormal MRI was 19 percent. However, if the girl was between ages 6 and 8, the chance of an abnormal MRI was only 2 percent. Of the eleven girls in the study with abnormal MRIs, the most common finding, in six girls, was a hypothalamic hamartoma, a small, nonmalignant developmental malformation that can result in very rapid progression of puberty but does not actually require surgery to remove it because it does not grow like a tumor. Only three girls had tumors, all of which were malignant gliomas, including one in a girl who was nearly 8 years old and had no neurological signs of a brain tumor.

When I first read this article, I was pleased that the chances of missing an abnormal finding on MRIs in girls who started puberty between ages 6 and 8 was so small. To me, this indicated that the guidelines I had helped develop were very reasonable, since clearly precocious puberty in the vast majority of 6-to-8-year-old girls was idiopathic. This would tend to support the view that these girls are almost all normal children who start maturing at the early end of what I would consider the normal range for female puberty. However, the authors of the study saw things differently. They argued that to miss even one girl with a brain tumor was too many, so they set about trying to find other criteria that would help identify the small proportion of girls with abnormal MRIs. Most of the hormone tests they looked at were not helpful, but they concluded that the girls with hamartomas or tumors had somewhat higher estradiol levels than the idiopathic girls, although there was a lot of overlap. To make sure that every girl with an abnormal MRI was identified, they stated that they would have needed to do MRIs on the 50 percent of the girls with precocious puberty who had the highest estradiol levels. In the language of epidemiology, the finding of a high estradiol level was sensitive (i.e., it detected all the girls with abnormal MRIs) but not very specific (i.e., it also applied to about half of the girls with normal MRIs). They argued that further studies needed to be done to more accurately identify predictors of abnormal MRIs in early-maturing girls. After all, there is no guarantee that what is true for French girls (mostly white in this study) would apply to early-maturing U.S. girls, a large proportion of whom are black.

I wrote an editorial that accompanied this article, titled "Precocious Puberty in Girls and the Risk of a Central Nervous System Abnormality: The Elusive Search for Diagnostic Certainty."[2] I argued that the authors had made a major contribution by providing solid data on the risk of an abnormal MRI in girls with precocious puberty based on their age. I expressed skepticism, based on the problems I mentioned in interpreting estradiol measurements in labs in the United States, that measuring this hormone would prove to be of much use in distinguishing idiopathic from nonidiopathic precocious puberty. I also pointed out that to be 100 percent certain that a girl with precocious puberty did *not* have a tumor or a hamartoma, one would really need to do an MRI on *all* girls who started having breast development before age 8, even though the chances of finding something in girls over 6 is only around 2 percent. The strategy I favor is to do an MRI on all girls starting puberty before age 6 and on selected girls who are over age 6. I would recommend it if they have any symptoms of a brain abnormality (such as headaches or visual changes) or if their puberty is advancing unusually rapidly. This approach will spare most early-maturing girls and their parents the anxiety of undergoing a head MRI, which can be very stressful, not to mention expensive. I must add that it would not have identified one 7-year-old girl in the French study with a glioma, so parents need to be aware that the risk of a brain tumor in a 6-to-8-year-old with early puberty and no neurological symptoms, while very low, is not zero. However, the most common MRI finding in the French study was the hamartoma, which would not cause major problems if it was missed because it does not grow and there is no need to remove it. Most parents I have talked to seem to understand that it is difficult to justify doing an MRI routinely in situations where the risk is very low. After all, it is not considered necessary to do an MRI on every child with headaches unless the clinical picture (headaches becoming more frequent and more severe over time) suggests an increased risk of finding something abnormal.

My advice to parents whose daughter has signs of early puberty and whose physician recommends a head MRI is twofold. First, don't agree to schedule the MRI until the hormone testing is completed. Sometimes the GnRH testing either will be equivocal or will show clearly that the problem is not central precocious puberty, in which case the rationale for doing the MRI simply does not exist. Further follow-up may be needed before a clear diagnosis can be made. Second, if the child has seen a specialist who is certain that the problem is central precocious puberty based on hormone testing and the child is older than 6, then you need to decide how much uncertainty you are willing to live with. If you will not sleep well knowing that there is only a 2 percent chance that something will show up, you should go ahead with the MRI. One drawback of this approach, however, is that MRIs can detect very small changes in the area of the pituitary gland or hypothalamus that may be variants of normal and have nothing whatsoever to do with the child's puberty. So if you agree to do the MRI, prepare yourself for the possible need to do another one to be sure that any minor abnormality that might be detected is not changing over time. If you decide not to do the MRI, you should still keep any follow-up appointment that the specialist suggests. In the event that the progression of puberty becomes very rapid or new brain-related symptoms (headaches, change in vision) develop, there is still time to find whatever is there and have it managed appropriately before any more serious problems develop.

CHAPTER 8

TO TREAT OR NOT TO TREAT?
THAT IS THE QUESTION

We have finally arrived at what I feel to be the critical question regarding girls with early puberty: In what cases should they be treated with medications to stop or slow the progression? There are cases that all of the specialists in my field would feel very comfortable treating, and others that very few of us would treat. What makes this a troublesome issue, however, is that in my experience there are a lot of young girls with signs of early puberty where the opinion a parent will be given on treatment will depend a great deal on the particular physician who is giving it. Before I delve into the specifics of this debate, I will first need to review the history of therapy for precocious puberty.

HISTORICAL PERSPECTIVE

The history of the treatment of precocious puberty is well reviewed in an excellent article by Boepple, et al.[1] It was first recognized in the 1950s that there was a need for medications that would inhibit production of gonadotropins as a means for controlling sexual precocity and other states of overactivity of the gonads. In 1962, medroxyprogesterone acetate (MPA), a modified version of progesterone better known by the name Depo-Provera, was first shown to be successful in treating central precocious puberty. Progesterone is the hormone made by the ovary during the second half of the menstrual cycle, which helps prepare the uterus to receive the fertilized egg from the fallopian tube and sustain pregnancy. If a fertilized egg does not attach itself to the lining of the uterus, the corpus luteum (the structure that makes progesterone) regresses, progesterone levels fall, and the lining of the uterus is shed, resulting in menstrual flow. One of the actions of progesterone is to suppress the production of gonadotropins, which is the basis for its well-known contraceptive action. When given over the long term by intramuscular injection every two weeks, MPA was effective in preventing menses or stopping it in girls who had already started, and it prevented further increases in breast development. However, subsequent studies showed that MPA did not do a very good job of slowing rapid growth and the rapid rate of skeletal maturation in young girls with precocious puberty. Thus, these girls remained at risk for short adult stature, one of the major reasons for treating this condition. Another problem with MPA was that as investigators tried to use larger doses to obtain better results, there was evidence of a suppression of the functioning of the adrenal gland, presumably due to MPA having at large doses a cortisone-like action.

During the 1970s, important work was being done in animals such as monkeys to better understand how GnRH regulates the production of LH and FSH by the pituitary gland. The striking outcome of years of careful study was that the pituitary gland would respond to GnRH with the release of gonadotropins only if the GnRH was either secreted by the hypothalamus or given by the researcher in a pulsatile fashion. The ideal spacing of the pulses was one to two hours apart. In one notable study, a group of scientists in Pittsburgh led by Dr. Ernest Knobil tried to restart puberty in monkeys whose hypothalamus had been damaged, by giving GnRH continuously directly into a vein. Regardless of how much GnRH they gave, LH and FSH production remained low, but as soon as they started delivering the GnRH by pulses, LH and FSH began to rise and soon became normal.[2] Soon similar studies were being done on human subjects who were unable to produce gonadotropins, and again the pulsatile administration of GnRH was found to be effective in helping men who had been unable to make LH and FSH produce them normally and even become fertile.

GnRH was first discovered and purified in the early 1970s, and it was found to be a very short protein (called a peptide) consisting of only ten amino acids. Once the sequence of the amino acids had been determined, investigators began the process of synthesizing slightly altered forms of GnRH that they hoped would be more potent (meaning that less of the protein would be needed to get the same effect) and longer-lasting. When the original or native form of GnRH is injected into an animal or a person, it stays in the circulation for only a few minutes because enzymes in the blood break it down very quickly. Producing an altered form of GnRH that would not be broken down so quickly seemed like a good idea, since one would then not need to give it so often. After some trial and error, scientists ended up with a number of modified forms of GnRH that both were more potent (meaning they had a stronger attraction for their receptor on the surface of the gonadotropes) and resisted degradation in the blood (which meant they would last a lot longer). When these modified forms of GnRH, which are referred to as GnRH analogs, were given to patients who were unable to make gonadotropins (presumably due to a lack of GnRH), they failed to consistently increase gonadotropins. In fact, after a while, the pituitary became resistant to the drugs, because they blocked rather than stimulated the release of LH and FSH. We now know that this occurs because the pituitary responds only to pulses of GnRH, and long-acting GnRH analogs expose the pituitary to constant stimulation. Somewhere along the line, some bright investigators realized that while long-acting GnRH analogs might be useless for patients with gonadotropin deficiency, they might be just what was needed for patients with precocious puberty.

Clinical trials with GnRH analogs in girls and boys with precocious puberty began in the Developmental Endocrinology Branch at the NIH in Bethesda, Maryland, in the late 1970s and at the Reproductive Endocrine Unit at Massachusetts General Hospital (MGH) in Boston. The medication was given by the parents as a subcutaneous injection once a day. The first report, published in the *New England Journal of Medicine* in 1981 by the group at the NIH, was quite impressive.[3] It showed that after giving the drug for eight weeks, the response of the pituitary to an IV injection of native GnRH (which, as you recall, is very brisk in central precocious puberty, especially for LH) was completely inhibited and levels of sex steroids fell to levels normal for prepubertal children. Furthermore, when the drug was stopped, hormone levels rapidly rose back to baseline within eight weeks, indicating the drug had no long-term effect on the reproductive axis. As these patients were followed for up to two years, it became clear that the rapid growth rate soon slowed to normal, and most important of all, the rapid increase in skeletal maturation was either greatly slowed or in some cases brought to a screeching halt.[4] On the average, bone age advanced only half a year for every year of treatment, whereas before treatment, the bone age typically advanced more than two years per year. Further follow-up of these patients for five to six years showed that the positive effects of treatment were maintained, and a dramatic improvement in predicted height (due to continued slowing of bone age maturation) was demonstrated.

While studies in children with precocious puberty were continuing at the NIH and the MGH, a drug company finally brought one of the synthetic GnRH analogs, leuprolide acetate or Lupron, to market. Curiously, it was initially marketed not for precocious puberty but for men with prostate cancer! This puzzled me at first, but there was a logical explanation. Prostate cancer is known to be very dependent on testosterone for growth, so lowering testosterone levels in the blood would be expected to help slow tumor growth. The simplest way to do this would be to surgically remove the testes, but it was felt that men might more readily accept a medical way to accomplish the same end. GnRH analogs, by desensitizing the pituitary to stimulation by GnRH, suppress LH, FSH, and sex steroids in men the same way they do in young girls. The reason it was marketed first for men was economics: There are many more men out there needing treatment for prostate cancer than young girls and boys needing treatment for precocious puberty. Eventually, clinical trials on Lupron for children with precocious puberty were started, and after enough data were submitted to the FDA by TAP Pharmaceuticals, Lupron in the form of a daily injection was officially approved for use in children.

Meanwhile, two further advances in GnRH analog therapy were reported. Several groups were testing a preparation that could be given by squirting it into a child's nose, thus avoiding the need for daily injection. The intranasal form of GnRH analogs was found to be as effective in suppressing gonadotropin secretion as the injectable form, but the drug needed to be given three to six times a day.[5] A more significant advance came in the late 1980s, when several groups reported the short-term results of treatment with a new form of Lupron called Lupron Depot, in which the drug was encapsulated into microspheres that, when suspended in a liquid and injected into the muscle, would release the active drug slowly over a period of at least a month.[6] By the early 1990s, long-term studies had clearly shown that monthly injections of Lupron Depot were effective in suppressing gonadotropin secretion and slowing both growth and skeletal maturation in children with central precocious puberty.[7] By 1993, Lupron Depot had been approved by the FDA for use in such children.

The approval of Lupron Depot was greeted with enthusiasm by the pediatric endocrine community, because a treatment was now available that would not require parents to learn to give daily injections of medication at home, as the monthly injections could easily be given in the office of either the specialist who prescribed it or the primary-care physician. Even so, some pediatric endocrinologists were already sounding a note of caution on the widespread use of this new therapy. Two articles that appeared in 1994 are particularly worthy of comment. The first, a report by two researchers at the University of Michigan, attempted to answer the question of how much effect treatment with GnRH analogs really had on adult height, particularly when one considered the age at which treatment was started.[8] You should recall that in chapter 3, I discussed the fact that some older studies had reported that the majority of girls with central precocious puberty reached an adult height within the normal range without any treatment at all. Drs. Kletter and Kelch did what we call a *retrospective study* in which they invited pediatric endocrinologists in the U.S. and Europe to submit data on girls who had been treated for central precocious puberty as well as girls with the same diagnosis who had not been treated, but whose adult heights were known. They then put together all the data and divided the girls into two groups according to the age at which they were diagnosed: before 6 years and after 6 years. A summary of their results is shown in Table 6.

Two points should be noted. One is that in this group of patients, a positive effect on adult height was noted in the group started at a younger age, but this was a relatively small group and the effect on adult height of those treated did not

TABLE 6: EFFECT OF TREATMENT TO SUPRESS EARLY PUBERTY
ON FINAL HEIGHT ACCORDING TO AGE AT DIAGNOSIS

	Age less than 6 at diagnosis		Age greater than 6 at diagnosis	
	Treated	Control	Treated	Control
Number of girls	17	10	114	54
Average age	4.7	4.6	8.1	8.3
Average final height	5'3¼"	5'1½"	5'2"	5'1¾"

Adapted from Kletter and Kelch, *J. Clin. Endocrinol. Metab.* 1994; 79:331–334.

seem to be very large. In the older group, the effect of treatment on adult height was virtually nil, but it is noteworthy that the average age at time of treatment was just over 8 years, suggesting that many of the girls had puberty that was borderline precocious or not truly precocious at all, using the old definition of when puberty in girls is precocious. The following year, a study was published from a group of endocrinologists in San Francisco in which most of the girls started treatment before age 5, and they agreed that the effects of treatment on final height in the younger girls was more impressive than in girls who were started on treatment after age 5.[9]

The second article was written by Dr. Robert Rosenfield at the University of Chicago, the same Dr. Rosenfield mentioned on page 6 who led the group of endocrinologists unhappy about the new puberty guidelines.[10] It is based on a talk he gave at a symposium on precocious puberty in 1993, not long after Lupron Depot and two other similar drugs were approved by the FDA for precocious puberty. I will quote him here because he articulates the key issues well, and on the issue of treatment he and I are in full agreement. He states right up front:

These agents have the potential to be overprescribed. Consequently, it is important that physicians understand the place of these agents in the management of precocious puberty . . . [and] . . . one must ask the following questions to avoid inappropriate GnRH analog treatment.

1) Is puberty premature?
2) Are sex hormone levels pubertal and dependent on gonadotropins?

3) Is puberty rapidly progressive and is height potential compromised?
4) Is psychosocial well-being currently or potentially compromised by the precocity?
5) Will the quality of life be improved by this therapy?
6) What are the unknowns of GnRH therapy?

Is Puberty Premature?

Although Dr. Rosenfield and I may differ in our view of the age at which puberty should be considered premature, there is no doubt that even using the old definition of precocious puberty, many girls are being treated who are early maturers (e.g., 8–9 years of age) but not precocious, as can be seen from the ages of the girls in the older group in the table. Although many physicians have assumed and informed parents that such early maturers will benefit from treatment in terms of their ultimate height, this is apparently not true. A recent study from Israel specifically looked at girls with pubertal onset between ages 8 and 9 who were progressing rapidly. Half of the parents agreed to treatment with GnRH analogs, which continued for two to four years, while the other half declined and were followed as controls. The treated group progressed through puberty more slowly than the controls and had menses at 12.8 versus 10.8 years, but the average adult height in both groups was just under 5 feet 2 inches.[11]

Is It Gonadotropin-Dependent?

To be sure that the pubertal changes one sees are dependent on gonadotropins, one either needs to be sure that unstimulated LH and FSH levels are clearly elevated or, preferably, have the girl undergo a GnRH stimulation test, as described in chapter 7. Dr. Rosenfield emphasized that GnRH analogs are not effective in treating forms of sexual precocity that are not gonadotropin-dependent, such as premature adrenarche.

Is It Rapidly Progressive?

To quote Dr. Rosenfield, "If puberty is not rapidly progressive, GnRH therapy is not required. Although normal puberty is progressive once it begins, precocious puberty is not necessarily progressive or rapidly progressive. Precocious puberty occurs on a spectrum ranging from typical benign premature thelarche through nonprogressive or slowly progressive complete precocity to rapidly progressive complete precocity. *Longitudinal assessment of the tempo of puberty is thus necessary in all children with premature puberty*" (italics added). Dr. Rosenfield referred to two studies, one of which he coauthored, which showed that "children identified as having a nonprogressive or slowly progressive course, even though they may reach the point of menarche, do not have a compromised height potential."[12] Further studies published in 1999 and 2000 described additional young girls whose puberty progressed slowly or not at all during follow-up, were not treated with GnRH analogs, and achieved adult heights consistent with their genetic potential.[13,14] One study reported the average age of menarche in these girls at 11 years, and in another it was nearly 12 years, so it is clear that early appearance of breast tissue does not by itself indicate that menses will start very early. The problem, as one expert in the field stated, is that no single test will reliably identify those 5-to-8-year-old girls who will progress rapidly and need treatment compared to those who will do well if left alone.[15] A bone age advanced by two years or more or an LH-predominant GnRH test helps, but even some patients with those characteristics progress slowly during follow-up. The best approach is for these children to be followed closely by a specialist without treatment, with physical exams, growth measurements, and repeat bone age studies at six-to-twelve-month intervals. Those girls who clearly have a progressive increase in breast size, rapid growth, rapid advancement of bone maturation, and a significant decrease in the height prediction or a predicted height of less than five feet are the ones who should be treated.

Psychosocial Well-Being

Dr. Rosenfield reviewed some of the studies I discussed in chapter 3 concerning the modest increase in behavioral problems in girls with precocious puberty, but he concludes that "the extent to which GnRH analog treatment would be helpful in regard to these psychosocial problems is unknown." That is still the case today.

Will Treatment Improve Quality of Life?

Stopping menses, with "its potential to stress both the child and her caretakers," is viewed as a major advantage of treatment. He also points out that GnRH may not be necessary in children with central precocious puberty complicating a neurological disorder causing profound mental retardation. In such children, who are unable to maintain proper menstrual hygiene, stopping periods is a real benefit, but since growth and adult height are not of concern, one can accomplish the same objective by using monthly

Depo-Provera injections at about 5 percent of the cost of GnRH analog treatment.

Unknowns and Side Effects of GnRH Therapy

Dr. Rosenfield pointed out that there was still much we did not know about the long-term effects of GnRH therapy, including any effects on ultimate fertility. As I write this, more than eight years later, reports of serious side effects of Lupron therapy have been few. The most common problem associated with treatment is a type of local reaction to the injection called a sterile abscess, since it can look like an infection but there are no bacteria inside. TAP Pharmaceuticals states this has been a problem in 5 percent of patients taking Lupron Depot. Since menses either start or resume six to twelve months after stopping Lupron, one could assume that effects on fertility will not be common. However, once enough treated children have been followed well into adulthood, it is still possible that we will see an increased frequency of problems with fertility or with the reproductive axis in women. The potential for rare and delayed reactions is present for nearly any medication taken over a prolonged period of time. In my view, if the potential benefit of treatment is great, a small risk is worth taking, but if the benefit is borderline or questionable, that small risk may not be worth taking. Dr. Rosenfield makes one more excellent point when he states that "it seems particularly important to consider the psychological unknowns. The treatment and requisite frequent evaluations might themselves create a poor self-image and foster the psychosocial maladjustment so frequently associated with chronic disease." I believe that parents who have a generally healthy and happy 7-to-9-year-old with early puberty should give serious thought to how the child might react to monthly shots and visits to the specialist for a physical exam, including breast measurement and blood tests, every three to four months. There is to my knowledge no study that has specifically looked at how young girls cope emotionally with the stresses of being treated for precocious puberty, especially those who do not see their early breast development as a big deal (and I have seen many such girls). However, I would not be surprised if the treatment were shown to *cause* as many behavior problems in young girls as it alleviates.

HOW I APPROACH THE DECISION TO TREAT OR NOT TO TREAT

Over the past ten years, since Lupron Depot became available and made treatment of central precocious puberty a lot less stressful for families, I have seen hundreds of girls referred for suspected precocious puberty, and I do not think I have treated more than ten. One reason is that only about 10 percent of the girls I have seen have true precocious puberty, with most of the remainder having premature adrenarche or premature thelarche. Another reason is that many of these girls have been 7 or 8 years old, which is slightly precocious by the old definition and early but not precocious by the new guidelines. In these situations, I have a talk with the parents and the child to find out what potential problems they are most concerned about; if I can allay those concerns without drug therapy, they usually opt for no treatment. The third reason is that I am fairly conservative and cautious about the decision to commit a young girl and her family to a prolonged course of treatment costing at least $8,000 per year. If I end up recommending treatment, I want to feel pretty sure that starting the child on treatment is going to make a difference for her and her caretakers. If she has only a small amount of breast tissue (what we call Tanner stage 2) and it is the first time I am seeing her, how can I tell if her puberty is rapidly progressive, slowly progressive, or nonprogressive? Some in my field believe that ordering a battery of blood tests and X rays will answer that question, but as discussed earlier, there is no test that will reliably predict which girls will progress rapidly and which will not. I am convinced that the best way to proceed is to do no tests or a minimum of testing and re-examine the child in four to six months. That is sufficient time to detect the enlargement of breast tissue and rapid rate of growth (3–4 inches per year versus 2 inches per year) that are characteristic of progressive puberty. If I see a child who at the first visit is well advanced into puberty (usually with Tanner stage 3 breast tissue) or has already started her periods (this happens every so often), then the waiting period is not necessary and I start the testing at the first visit. However, most of the girls I have seen have been referred when the puberty is still in its early stages.

I have often seen young girls who were first seen by another specialist for the same problem and whose family either wanted a second opinion or had moved to my area and needed to find another pediatric endocrinologist. In quite a few cases, these girls had been started on Lupron or the parents had been told their daughter needed to be started, and in the majority I have recommended no treatment. In some cases, I thought that lab tests were not interpreted the way I would have, and did not clearly indicate central precocious puberty. But the most common reason I have disagreed with a decision to treat is that the child had only been seen once and had not been observed long enough to tell if the signs of puberty were progressing. When I saw these girls back four to six months later, the lack of significant progression convinced me I had made the right decision.

I often wonder why some of my colleagues are in such a rush to start girls on treatment before they are even sure what they are treating. It is not as though precocious puberty is like cancer and you have to "catch it early" or the child cannot be cured. If the signs of puberty are early, as they most often are, *there is no harm whatsoever in waiting four to six months or as long as necessary to accurately assess the rate of progression.* I always reassure parents that it typically takes at least two years after breasts appear for menses to start, and as noted above, some girls with slowly progressing or nonprogressive puberty may take as long as four to five years to start their menses. In the very rare event that a girl has her first period while being observed for progression, starting Lupron will suppress menses within a month. Some physicians may feel that since treatment is not harmful, it is preferable to treat some children who may not need it rather than follow them at intervals or let the parent and the primary-care physician keep an eye on things. If a child with a nonprogressive form of early puberty (e.g., premature thelarche) gets started on monthly injections, the parents and the treating physician will be very pleased four months later when the young girl looks exactly the same, and they will be convinced that the medication is really working. Of course, the same result would have been achieved had the child gotten monthly injections of sterile salt water or just been left alone! One can feel confident that a treatment is working only if there was something worth treating in the first place—specifically, enlarging breast tissue, rapid growth, and pubertal hormone levels. If a specialist recommends treatment for a girl with only a small amount of breast tissue with or without pubic hair and no clear increase in the rate of growth, my advice is to request a second opinion. Usually the child's primary-care physician will agree to this, and I have offered second opinions to many such families over the past twenty years.

TREATMENT CONSIDERATIONS

At present, the most common drug used to treat true precocious puberty is Lupron Depot, given as a monthly intramuscular injection, typically starting at a dose of 7.5 mg per month, though very large girls may need higher doses. A typical course of treatment lasts one to three years but may be longer in a child who is started at a very young age (less than 5). Once a child is started on treatment, hormone levels are suppressed into the prepubertal range within two months. Because it takes at least six weeks for the drug to have its full effect on the pituitary and ovaries, one should not be concerned if signs of puberty continue to progress for the first month. It is also not rare for the child to experience some vaginal bleeding during the first month of therapy due to hormone withdrawal. The amount of breast tissue may decrease somewhat, but it never goes away, and most often it remains unchanged during treatment. Experience has shown that 7.5 mg of Lupron per month is nearly always effective regardless of the weight of the child, though the drug manufacturer recommends a dose of 0.3 mg per kg of body weight, which means that 7.5 mg would be just right for a 25 kg (55 lb) child. For children weighing above 25 kg, many physicians will start on 11.25 mg per month (the next highest dose available), or even 15 mg for larger children, even though it is quite likely that the 7.5 mg dose will work just fine. The issue is not really safety but cost. At 7.5 mg per month, the cost usually works out to about $8,000 per year, and at the higher doses, the cost is correspondingly greater. (I should add that at least one study from France has recently appeared in which a depot preparation of Lupron 11.25 mg given only every three months, approved initially for adult women with certain gynecological problems, has been shown to be effective in suppressing puberty in children.[16] After additional studies are done to confirm this finding, this preparation may replace the monthly injections, with a significant increase in convenience for families.)

What should you do if the specialist recommends treatment and you do not have insurance or you do have insurance but the insurance company refuses to pay for the drug? Not many people have an extra $8,000 sitting around for this purpose, so it is difficult to cover the cost out of pocket. For people with no insurance, there are occasionally other ways to obtain the drug, which your doctor can check into if he or she feels strongly that the child needs treatment. Many HMOs carefully review requests for high-cost drugs such as growth hormone and Lupron and may request additional information from the treating physician before approving it. I have not encountered many cases where Lupron was denied, and when it is, it is usually because the child is older than the age at which puberty in a girl is considered precocious (for example, 9 or 10 years old). Whether or not you and the specialist should appeal the decision may depend on the doctor's assessment of the potential consequences of not treating it. If the decision to go ahead and treat was a close one, it may not be a bad idea to wait four to six months to see if the child's puberty progresses rapidly before deciding whether or not to pursue an appeal. If the drug was denied because the child was considered too old to need it, either accepting the decision or getting a second opinion should be considered.

During treatment, the specialist will usually want to see the child back every three to four months. One simple way to tell that the medication is working, in my experience, is to measure the child carefully and calculate the rate of growth since the last visit. If it is 2 inches per year or less, which is normal, the drug is probably having the desired effect. I also measure the amount of breast tissue with a ruler. If it has not grown since the last visit or has decreased, that is a good sign. The most accurate way to be sure that the medication is suppressing puberty, however, is to give an injection of GnRH and then measure LH and FSH thirty to sixty minutes later. In general, the peak LH and FSH should be much lower than before treatment, but depending on the method by which they are measured, different levels of LH and FSH will indicate if the medication is working or not.[17] Measuring estradiol levels is a much less accurate way to judge the effectiveness of treatment. If I can tell from the height and breast measurements that the medication is clearly working, I often dispense with the GnRH test. One problem with the test is that the dose of GnRH medication is expensive and often in short supply, and either the doctor needs to remember to order it or the patient has to bring a prescription to a pharmacy, have the pharmacy order it, pick it up, and bring it to the specialist at the time of the appointment. One group of physicians at Stanford University recently described a convenient shortcut for testing whether or not Lupron Depot is working. They found that the Lupron Depot preparation contains enough free drug (not bound to the microspheres) to increase LH and FSH within forty-five minutes of an injection, just like an injection of un-modified GnRH does.[18] Specialists can thus ask the parents to bring their monthly Lupron injection to their scheduled visit, have their nurse give it to the child, and then send the child to the lab to have blood drawn forty-five minutes later. This simple procedure saves money (not having to do a separate GnRH test), saves the child an extra needle, and seems to be as accurate as the standard GnRH test.

If measuring LH and FSH after giving GnRH or Lupron shows that the levels are still too high, the physician will often increase the Lupron Depot dose to the next strength (e.g., from 7.5 mg to 11.25 mg) and redo the test at a subsequent visit. If the LH and FSH levels are still not suppressed fully, it could mean the child requires a still higher dose of medication. I have, however, heard of situations where even very high doses of Lupron failed to suppress the puberty hormones completely. In such cases, I would wonder if the diagnosis is really true precocious puberty. If the child is thought to have true precocious puberty but actually has premature thelarche or premature adrenarche, even high doses of medication may not completely suppress the LH and FSH, and the treatment will accomplish nothing at all. Thus if the physician keeps recommending higher doses of medication, especially if the signs of puberty were fairly minimal when treatment was started, parents should not be shy about questioning the need for continued treatment. Getting a second opinion might be a good idea.

CHAPTER 9

CASE HISTORIES

I n this final chapter, I would like to give the reader an idea of how many of the issues I have discussed in this book apply to some of the patients I have seen in my practice. All of these accounts are taken directly from my patient files, and I have only altered the girls' names. I hope that from the brief description at the beginning of each case, parents of girls who already have signs of puberty will be able to find one that is similar to what their daughter is experiencing. Each case is accompanied by some comments on what key points I think they illustrate.

BREAST DEVELOPMENT
IN A 16-MONTH-OLD

Victoria was 16 months old when she was referred to me because her primary-care physician noted some breast tissue at her 15-month well-child visit and was concerned that she might be starting puberty. According to her mother, it had been there for a month or two. She was a healthy child who was on no medications. Her mother had had her first period at age 14. The only notable finding on Victoria's examination was that she had what felt like normal breast tissue under both nipples that was just under 1 inch in diameter. There was no pubic hair. Her height and weight were just above the 75th percentile on the growth chart, but at a year of age they had been at the 50th percentile, so there may have been more rapid growth than usual.

I explained to Victoria's mother that breast development in a healthy child under 3 years of age is almost always due to benign premature thelarche and not progressive precocious puberty. I decided not to order any lab tests or X rays but to see her back one more time in four months just to be certain. At her next visit, she was 20 months old. Her mother reported no change in the size of her breasts, but when I measured them, they had decreased to just over ½ inch in diameter. More important, she was growing at a normal rate and her height was still at the 75th percentile. With this new information, I told the mother that Victoria did not have precocious puberty and did not need any treatment. I pointed out that the breasts might increase or decrease slightly over the next year, but most likely they would disappear and not return until she was truly starting puberty in six to nine years. I told her I would be happy to see her again if I was wrong, but one and a half years later, I have heard from neither the mom nor her pediatrician.

I have seen so many cases of premature thelarche over the years that I feel very comfortable not ordering any tests when I am confident of the diagnosis. In most cases, I do not even see the child back for a second visit, but in such cases, I always ask the referring physician to let me know if puberty seems to be progressing.

PUBIC HAIR IN A 6-YEAR-OLD

Michelle was a black girl who was first seen by me at 6 years and 2 months of age. About six months earlier, the mother became concerned because she thought the child was developing breasts, and a month earlier, she noted some pubic hair and underarm odor. She went to her pediatrician, who concurred that she had breasts and pubic hair and suggested a referral. The mother was also concerned about her daughter's increased appetite and rapid weight gain. The family history was of note in that the mother was 5 feet 2 inches and weighed 193 pounds. She had her first period at age 11.

Michelle's height was at the 90th percentile, and when I reviewed the notes the pediatrician had sent me, I found that fifteen months earlier, her height had also been at the 90th percentile. Thus even though she was tall for her age, she was not growing too rapidly, as the mother believed. In the same period of time, her weight had increased from 60 to 73 pounds, and it was above the 95th percentile. I estimated that she was 25 percent overweight. When I examined her chest, I saw what appeared to be breast tissue, but when I carefully palpated it, it turned out to be entirely fat tissue. She did have pubic hair, which I rated at Tanner stage 2.

I concluded based on my exam that she had benign premature adrenarche. I told Michelle's mother that it was common for parents and even pediatricians to mistake fat tissue for breast tissue. Since she really had no breast development, she did not have puberty. I explained that the pubic hair came not from estrogens made by the ovaries but from weak androgens made by her adrenal glands. I pointed out that my research and the work of others suggested that early pubic hair was more likely to occur in overweight girls than in thin girls. As for tests, I could have ordered a DHEA-S to determine the level of the most abundant adrenal androgen, but I knew it would be mildly elevated and it would not have changed how I cared for the child. I told her I would need to see her again only if there was a rapid increase in pubic hair or the appearance of real breast tissue over the next year, and I have not heard from her since.

PUBIC HAIR STARTING AT AGE 7 ACCOMPANIED BY RAPID GROWTH

Lakisha was a black girl who was referred to me at age 7 because of rapid growth and recent appearance of pubic hair. The mother reported that she had always been tall for her age but had grown more rapidly in the past year. A year earlier, she had started having body odor and begun using deodorants. Six months earlier, pubic hair had appeared. Her mother was 5 feet 5 inches tall and began her periods at age 12. The father was 6 feet 3 inches tall, and the mother did not know about the timing of his puberty. The child had exercise-induced asthma and took medications only when she wheezed. She also had mild eczema, which was being treated with steroid cream. She was in the second grade and was the tallest in her class.

On her exam, her height was well above the 95th percentile and would have been average for a 10-year-old. Her weight was at the 95th percentile, so she was not overweight. Comparing my measurement with that done in her pediatrician's office a year earlier, she had grown 4 inches instead of the usual 2½ inches, so she was indeed growing rapidly. I could not find any breast tissue and there was stage 2 pubic hair, but the rest of her exam was completely normal. Because of her rapid growth, I did a few hormone tests, which showed that her DHEA-S was mildly elevated for her age, but everything else was normal. I ordered a bone age, which was equal to 10 years, about three years advanced. Because she was so tall, however, her adult height prediction was quite normal at 5 feet 6 inches, a bit taller than her mother.

Because of my concern for her rapid growth and to make sure I wasn't missing anything, I asked her to return to see me in five months, when she would be 7½. At that visit, her growth rate was still above normal (3 inches per year) but less rapid than it had been before. There was no breast tissue at all, and the amount of pubic hair had not increased. I reassured her mother that this was premature adrenarche and that she did not need any more tests or treatment unless things changed rapidly in the next year. A year later, while writing this chapter, I called the mother to see how Lakisha was doing. She was still growing rapidly, and the amount of pubic hair had increased only slightly, but two months earlier, the mother thought she had seen some breast tissue. I offered to see her again, and indeed she had early breast development and was still growing rapidly. At this point she was 8½ years old, and her age at starting breast development was early but not precocious by either the old definition or the new one. I reassured the mother that she would likely not start her periods until age 10½ or later, that her adult height would still be normal, and that the best thing we could do would be to leave her alone. The mother and Lakisha agreed that that was the best course.

Lakisha is an example of accelerated growth and bone

maturation in an otherwise typical case of premature adrenarche. Many of my colleagues and I are seeing such girls (as well as boys with similar growth patterns), and over the past three years, eight of forty-eight cases (17 percent) of premature adrenarche I have seen have had a period of rapid growth starting as early as 4–5 years of age. All had bone ages advanced by at least two years but normal predicted height. The first question we ask is what is causing the rapid growth and bone maturation, since the amount of adrenal androgens made do not seem to be sufficient to cause this. We do not know for sure, but it is possible that these children's bones are more sensitive to stimulation of growth by the modest levels of adrenal androgens they produce. The second question is what, if anything, we should do about it. In our online discussions, a few doctors in my field have advocated treating girls like Lakisha with Lupron, figuring that it ought to slow the rapid bone age advancement the way it does in true precocious puberty. The problem is that Lupron has no direct effect that we know of on bone maturation. It works only if elevated levels of gonadotropins are driving the ovaries to make enough estrogens to speed growth and bone maturation. Given the lack of breast tissue in these girls, it is doubtful that their pituitary glands are stimulating their ovaries to make estrogens, and therefore a drug that suppresses the pituitary's production of gonadotropins would not have any effect. Given that children with advanced bone maturation tend to start puberty earlier than most children, it is not surprising that Lakisha started to have breast development not long after she turned 8, since by that time her bone age was about 11½. What has been published on the subject suggests that most girls like this will end up neither tall nor short, but close to the height one would predict based on the heights of their parents.

DISAPPEARING AND REAPPEARING
BREAST DEVELOPMENT
IN A 6-YEAR-OLD

Deborah was a 6-year-old white girl whom I saw about two months after her mother had noted a knot under her left nipple. Curiously, her mother felt that the amount of breast tissue had actually decreased in the interval between her first finding it and my seeing her. Deborah was a healthy child who was on no medications. The mother had no history of early breast development and her periods had started at age 13½. A 7-year-old sister had no breast development.

On my examination, her height was at the 50th percentile and had been at the 50th percentile at least since age 4. Her weight was at the 75th percentile. Her exam was completely normal except that there was a ½-inch button of breast tissue under her left nipple but nothing under her right nipple. There was no pubic hair and the vagina looked normal.

I explained to the mother that Deborah could have either premature thelarche (though she was older than most girls I have seen with that diagnosis) or very early precocious puberty. I felt that doing lab tests and X rays would not be helpful, since regardless of what they showed, I was going to wait to see what happened before taking any action. I told her mother that I did not think she was going to progress over the next year but to contact me if there was a significant increase in breast size over the next year.

I heard nothing further, but while writing this book, I decided to check in with Deborah's mother to see if anything had changed. It was now eighteen months later, and Deborah would be 7½. When I told her mother why I had called, she said, "It's funny that you called, because I was thinking about bringing her back to see you." She related that the small amount of breast tissue I had detected on my exam had disappeared completely not long thereafter. Her growth had been at a normal rate, according to her pediatrician. However, three weeks before I called, the child had noted some tenderness and swelling, this time under her *right* nipple. I offered to see her again, and the mother commented that it would probably disappear before she got to me. I told her that now that she was 7½ years old, it was possible that she was in very early puberty this time, but we would know better if the right breast continued to grow over the next four to six months and the left one started too. I also pointed out that if Deborah appeared to be in early puberty but it did not seem to be progressing very rapidly, I might advise just watching it. As in the next case, that of Laura, 7-to-8-year-old girls starting puberty often do fine with reassurance and without any treatment.

This case illustrates a pattern we see occasionally: Girls with early breast development that not only does not progress but actually disappears and reappears at a later time. For reasons we do not understand, having breast tissue on one side but not the other is fairly common in such cases. However, breast development on one side only in a 6-year-old can also be the first sign of true precocious puberty that progresses rapidly, as illustrated later, in the case of Rochelle. I believe that the best approach in these young girls is to avoid doing a lot of tests, which may confuse the situation, and explain to the parents that more time is needed to determine whether the child has a progressive form of precocious puberty, which will require testing and possibly treatment.

PRECOCIOUS PUBERTY STARTING AT AROUND AGE 7 AND NOT TREATED

Laura was an 8-year-old white girl whom I saw for a second opinion on treatment of her precocious puberty. She had initially been seen by another endocrinologist at age 6 years 7 months. There was thought to be a very small amount of breast tissue, but her LH and estradiol were low, and it was recommended that nothing be done. At a follow-up visit six months later, no progression was noted. However, at age 7 years 9 months, it appeared that her breasts were somewhat larger. Her bone age was about one and a half years advanced. The endocrinologist wanted to order further tests and start treatment, but Laura's grandparents, who had raised her since birth, were skeptical that treatment was necessary and asked for another opinion. Three months later, just before her eighth birthday, I met Laura and her grandparents.

Her height was between the 75th and 90th percentiles, whereas it had been just above the 50th percentile at age 6 years 7 months. Thus there was evidence that her growth rate was increased. Her breast development was between Tanner stages 2 and 3, and she had no pubic hair. We discussed the pros and cons of treating what I felt was progressive true precocious puberty, starting most likely at between ages 7 and 7½. I explained that this was at the early end of what we now consider the broad normal range for onset of puberty. I predicted based on her bone age that she would end up between 5 feet 1 inch and 5 feet 4 inches, so they were not too concerned about her growth. Laura was in third grade but was a very outgoing child who was not at all bothered by her breast development. She was emphatic in telling us that she did not want to take shots to stop her puberty. I predicted that without any treatment, she would probably start her periods between 9½ and 10 years of age. The grandparents felt that they could handle this when the time came, and thanked me for supporting their decision not to pursue treatment with Lupron.

Two years later, while writing this book, I called the grandparents to find out how things had turned out. To prepare Laura for starting her periods, her grandmother had bought her a book called *The Care and Keeping of You: A Body Book for Girls*, which Laura enjoyed. When Laura was 9½, she came to her grandmother one evening with blood on her panties. She was told that her periods had started and that it happens to everyone, but she was just a bit earlier than most. Laura began to cry and said, "I really don't want this." Her grandmother went out to find some pads and a while later brought home five different kinds to make sure one would be right for Laura. When she returned, she was surprised to find that Laura had prepared a party for her and her grandfather, and told them, "Now I understand that this is a day for rejoicing, not for crying." Since then, Laura has been managing her periods very well and quickly gotten used to wearing pads. At first she told her grandmother as soon as they started, but after a few months, she waited three days before telling her, and then announced, "I just wanted to let you know that I could handle it." I asked Laura's grandmother how things were going at school. Laura was the first in her class to start having periods, but another girl started a few months later. By this time, her breasts had developed to the point where they were easily noticed, and one girl remarked to her, "You've really got yourself some big boobs."

Laura replied without embarrassment, "Your day will come." The grandmother helped out in class from time to time, and several parents commented to her that they couldn't believe how much Laura had developed; one remarked that she just dreaded that this was going to happen to her daughter too. When I asked the grandmother why she thinks Laura adjusted so well, she said, "A lot depends on how the parents accept it and present it to the child."

This case illustrates that in a supportive family environment, many girls who start puberty at an age that in the past was clearly considered precocious will manage fine without treatment. The calmer and more reassuring the parents can be, the more likely it is that the young girl will adjust to early breast development and early periods. I suspect that in situations like this, some parents who are very anxious to start the injections are worried as much about how they will cope as they are about how their daughter will cope. Of course, every family situation is unique, and there are certainly girls who are more withdrawn and less mature than Laura was, who would have a very difficult time handling periods at age 9½ with the grace Laura showed.

PRECOCIOUS PUBERTY STARTING AT
AGE 6½ AND TREATED WITH LUPRON

Kelly was a 7½-year-old white girl referred to me for evaluation of early breast development. Her mother told me that her two concerns were that Kelly would start her menses very early and that she would stop growing too soon. She had first noted breast budding when Kelly was about 6½ years old, and six months later pubic hair and body odor appeared. All of these had increased over the past six months. The mother also felt that she had been growing more rapidly for at least six months. Kelly's mother had had menarche at age 9, so she was obviously an early maturer herself, but she had reached a height of 5 feet 4 inches. Kelly was in the second grade and was doing fine but admitted to feeling somewhat embarrassed about the changes to her body.

She was 4 feet 5½ inches, which for her age was slightly above the 95th percentile. I did not have growth records from the doctor who referred her, but given that she was quite tall for her age, it seemed plausible that she was growing rapidly. Her weight was more above the 95th percentile than her height, so she was somewhat overweight. The only other noteworthy part of her exam was that her breasts and pubic hair were already at Tanner stage 3. It is unusual for girls to have breast development that advanced at their first visit. I checked her LH and FSH, and even without stimulation by GnRH, it was clear that the levels were pubertal. Estradiol was also in the pubertal range. Her bone age was 10½ years, or three years advanced, confirming that puberty was progressing rapidly. Her predicted height based on her bone age was about 5 feet 2 inches.

Given that her breast development was already fairly advanced by age 7½, I felt that without treatment, she would likely start having periods before age 9, which, while consistent with her mother's history of early menses, was probably more than she would be able to cope with. Therefore, I recommended that we get her started on monthly injections of Lupron 7.5 mg to slow the rapid progression of her puberty. I did not feel that an MRI to rule out a brain tumor was necessary since with puberty starting after age 6 and no neurological symptoms, the risk of finding something was low.

Her first injection of Lupron was given in the office of her primary-care physician three weeks later. Three weeks after that, she had some vaginal bleeding, which lasted for about ten days, but there were no further episodes. Four months later, she returned for her first follow-up visit. Her mother was pleased to report that she was more cheerful and less temperamental. The mother was concerned, however, that she had started having occasional headaches after the Lupron was started, and they had gotten worse during the three weeks before her visit. My exam showed that her growth had slowed significantly, and there was no change in the amount of breast tissue or pubic hair. Her neurological exam was normal. I had the lab draw an LH level forty-five minutes after she got her Lupron injection, and the level was suppressed, as I had anticipated. However, because of the worsening headaches, I ordered an MRI to make sure there was no tumor. Fortunately, the study was negative. At her next visit four months later, the mother told me the headaches had resolved not long after her MRI, and she suspected they had been stress-related. The amount of breast tissue had decreased slightly and her growth was still slow. The next two follow-up visits were uneventful, and due to the slowing of her growth, her height was now on the 90th percentile. There was little change in her breast and pubic hair development and no periods. Her weight had increased to the point where, based on the drug company's recommended dose, I could have prescribed the 11.25 mg or even the 15 mg dosage, but she did just fine with the 7.5 mg dose I had started her on. At the visit just after her ninth birthday,

Kelly expressed the wish to stop the monthly injections because she was getting tired of going to the doctor for them. Her mother and I agreed we would continue until she was about 9½, so that by the time she started her periods, she would be close to age 10 and likely to be able to cope with them.

This is a child who had idiopathic central precocious puberty starting at age 6½. Since she was white, starting puberty at that age was abnormally early even using the revised guidelines. Had the progression of puberty been very slow, I might not have recommended treating her, but with her advanced breast development, rapid growth, and advanced bone age, I sensed her menses would start before age 9 and that she and her mother would have had trouble coping with it. Her predicted height was within the normal range, so the treatment was not needed to prevent her from being too short. Given that her mother had started her menses at age 9, it seemed very likely that Kelly's early puberty had a genetic basis and was not due to a brain tumor or malformation. Thus I did not order an MRI until she began having headaches. She tolerated the treatment well except for having a period a few weeks after the first injection, which was likely due to the rapid decline in hormone levels once the treatment took effect. It was curious that the mother mentioned an improvement in her mood at her first visit after starting treatment, as she had not mentioned her being temperamental at the initial visit. Although some parents do note positive changes in their daughter's behavior following suppression of puberty, this is by no means a consistent observation, and I would not want parents to believe that Lupron will take care of whatever moodiness their child with early puberty might have.

PRECOCIOUS PUBERTY TREATED
AFTER THE ONSET OF MENSES

Rochelle was a healthy black girl who was first seen for evaluation of puberty at 6 years 2 months of age. At that time, all that was noted was some breast tissue under her right nipple, which had appeared two months earlier, but nothing on the left side. We learned that her mother had started having periods when she was 10 years old. She was already fairly tall, with her height at the 95th percentile. Her blood tests showed that her LH, FSH, and estradiol were all low, so it was not clear at this point that Rochelle had central precocious puberty. However, her bone age was advanced by about two and a half years. I decided that we needed to follow her to see if puberty was progressing slowly or rapidly, so the mother was asked to bring her back in six months. Six months later, she had grown about 2½ inches, which is a rapid rate of growth (5 inches per year). Curiously, her breasts had not changed at all, still measuring about 1 inch on the right and very little on the left. Her bone age had advanced to 10 years, and her predicted height was 5 feet 2 inches. It was decided that she needed to come back in a month to have a GnRH test. This did not actually get done until five months later, at which time she was 7 years 1 month old. Her growth rate had slowed, but both breasts had enlarged somewhat. The GnRH test showed a small rise in LH and a slightly greater increase in FSH, which was not the LH-predominant response I was looking for. Her estradiol was slightly increased. Given the uncertainty as to whether or not this was truly central precocious puberty, I elected to just watch her. Six months later, her growth again had been rapid, but there was no change in her breast development. Her LH and FSH were both low. At her next visit, five months later, her breasts were once more growing. She was 8 years old and already 4 feet 8 inches. She was the tallest girl in her second-grade class but said that she was not teased about either her height or her breast development. We discussed doing another GnRH test and possibly treating her with Lupron if the results warranted it, and the mother said she would think about it and get back to me.

I next heard from Rochelle's mother nine months later (age 8 years 9 months), when she called me about a week after Rochelle had her first period. She told me that Rochelle had not said anything to her for three days, and it was discovered only when her mother found bloodstains in the bed and on her panties. She tried to get Rochelle to wear a sanitary napkin, but Rochelle refused. By the time I saw her in my office a few weeks later, she had had a second period. After much urging, she agreed to wear a sanitary napkin. The mother told me that she had tried to prepare her for early periods but that the child had refused to talk about it. Normally a very quiet child, Rochelle seemed very sad and withdrawn at this visit. She had continued to grow rapidly and was now just over 4 feet 11 inches. We repeated her blood tests, and this time the LH and FSH were clearly in the pubertal range. Rochelle and her mother readily agreed to have her started on monthly injections of Lupron 7.5 mg. Two weeks after her first injection, she had another period, and then they stopped. A few months later, Rochelle seemed pleased that she didn't have to deal with her periods anymore. Her breasts had gotten smaller (from Tanner stage 4 to stage 3), and her growth had slowed significantly. Her mother noted that she didn't seem to get irritated as easily, and her schoolwork, which had slipped while she was having periods, had started to improve.

After we had been treating Rochelle with Lupron for ten months and she was 9 years 8 months old, we began to discuss how long we should continue the treatment. Rochelle was not ready to stop, since she didn't want to start having periods again. We decided to continue for another six months, until she was 10 years 2 months old, which was also the end of the school year. By that time, she had been taking the injections for sixteen months and had grown slowly, as is usually the case during Lupron therapy, to 5 feet 1½ inches. As she received her last injection, she cheerfully told me that she was looking forward to having periods. We scheduled one more visit for six months down the road. At that visit (age 10 years 8 months), I learned that Rochelle's periods had restarted three and a half months after her last Lupron injection, and she had had two more since. Her mother told me she was doing fine, in part because a few of her friends were also having periods. She noted no changes in her behavior or her emotional state since stopping the medication, and she was doing well in the fifth grade. She had reached 5 feet 2 inches, which was what we had predicted a few years earlier. Her mother was pleased with the results of the treatment because it had given Rochelle time to become emotionally mature enough to handle having periods.

This case illustrates several important points. First, it is sometimes very difficult to tell if a young girl is going to progress rapidly through puberty by looking at the lab tests. On three occasions, the LH and FSH appeared to be low, and yet growth was rapid and the bone age was advancing rapidly. Breast development increased in spurts, but not consistently. Should I have pressed the mother to start the child on treatment earlier, before she started having periods? Perhaps, but I was uncertain based on the lab tests that the treatment would work, and I thought she might have a small ovarian cyst rather than central precocious puberty. Even though the bone age was quite advanced, the child was growing rapidly, and her predicted height of 5 feet 2 inches was not alarming. Also, the mother did not seem overly concerned. By the time she had her first period, about two and a half years after her breasts started developing, it was clear that this was central precocious puberty, and treatment was undertaken. As expected, the periods stopped within a month, and continued to be controlled as long as we continued her monthly injections. While ideally treatment should have started sooner, no serious harm was done by waiting until she started her periods, and the sixteen months of treatment were clearly beneficial to Rochelle's emotional state. I believe that by age 10, most girls are able to handle menses much better than they are able to at age 9, and this case provides a good example of this. I also like to discuss with both the child and the parents the timing of stopping the medication at least six months before I intend to do so, so that I do not spring it on the family, and they have time to get used to the idea.

MENSES IN A 7½-YEAR-OLD GIRL WITH NO BREAST DEVELOPMENT

Latoria was referred to me shortly after she had had an episode of vaginal bleeding that lasted for three days and was mostly light but contained some clots of blood. It was preceded by one day of abdominal pain. When I heard about this case, I was worried that she had precocious puberty that had progressed so rapidly that the parents had not had a chance to get her evaluated before her menses started. She was a generally healthy child except for occasional asthma attacks. Her mother was quite overweight and had started her periods around age 10.

On exam, her height was at the 90th percentile and her weight was slightly above the 95th percentile. What was most striking was that I could not detect any breast tissue at all. Her abdominal exam was normal, and I could not feel any masses. Her vaginal exam revealed no fresh or dried blood and no evidence of trauma or infection. Her LH level was very low (prepubertal) and her estradiol was very slightly elevated.

I thought about the possibility of sexual abuse, but the child seemed very calm and appropriate and the mother could not think of anyone who would have had the chance to abuse her. The mother also had never seen her insert any objects into her vagina, and there was no sign of infection. I thought of doing an ultrasound to see if there was a tumor in her uterus (extremely rare) but decided to hold off and see if the problem recurred. When I saw her again five months later, she had not had any more vaginal bleeding. She had grown somewhat rapidly and had a tiny amount of breast tissue, but her exam was otherwise the same as before. I told the mother she would probably not have any more vaginal bleeding until she was well into puberty, at least two years down the road.

This is an example of premature menses, a condition I discussed in chapter 2, which is menstrual bleeding in girls who have not started puberty yet. The cause is unknown, but I have seen five cases in the past three years, so it may be more common than it was in the past. These girls need an endocrine evaluation, including blood tests and sometimes a pelvic ultrasound, but if the tests are normal, I believe that parents should be reassured that the condition is usually benign. They should be told, however, to bring the girl back to the specialist if the condition does not resolve on its own, or if there is persistent pain or discharge in the genital area.

―――――

I hope that in reading these case histories, parents of girls with signs of early puberty will find both useful information and reassurance that, by and large, these girls do well. A few really do benefit from treatment to slow puberty and either stop or prevent periods, but in most cases, a simple explanation as to what is going on will help alleviate much of the anxiety and uncertainty that parents and occasionally the girls themselves feel. I would like to thank the parents of these girls, particularly Laura's grandmother, for sharing with me what had occurred with their daughters a year or more after I last saw them. It is by listening to parents rather than just talking to them that I have learned the most about how to manage girls with early puberty in a calming and understanding way.

adrenal androgens—hormones made by the adrenal glands that cause the growth of pubic and axillary (underarm) hair

adrenarche—the time at which the increase in adrenal androgen production is first noted, typically by the appearance of pubic hair and body odor

body mass index (BMI)—an easily determined measure of fatness, calculated as the weight (in kg) divided by the height (in meters) squared

bone age—a measure of skeletal maturity, determined by taking an X ray of the hand and comparing it to an atlas of pictures of hand X rays of normal girls and boys

congenital adrenal hyperplasia—a genetic defect affecting the ability of the adrenal glands to produce cortisone, which can result in overproduction of adrenal androgens; in severe cases, girls have ambiguous genitalia at birth, but in mild cases, one can see early appearance of pubic hair and rapid growth, making it appear similar to premature adrenarche

DHEA, DHEA-S—abbreviations for the major circulating adrenal androgens, dehydroepiandrosterone and dehydroepiandrosterone sulfate

estradiol—the major estrogen made by the ovaries

estrogens—the general term for the female hormones, made by the ovaries, that stimulate breast development

follicle-stimulating hormone (FSH)—the pituitary hormone that stimulates the maturation of the egg follicles of the ovary and sperm production in the testes

gonadotropins—both LH and FSH, the puberty hormones of the pituitary gland, which stimulate the gonads

gonadotropin-releasing hormone (GnRH)—the hormone released from the part of the brain called the hypothalamus, which causes the pituitary gland to release LH and FSH

gonads—the ovaries or the testes

hamartoma—a developmental defect in the area of the hypothalamus that is occasionally found on brain imaging in girls with very early and rapidly progressive puberty

hypothalamic-pituitary-gonadal (HPG) axis—the working together of all three parts of the body to produce the hormonal and physical changes of puberty

hypothalamus—the part of the brain that makes GnRH, which signals the pituitary gland to produce the puberty hormones LH and FSH

insulin—the hormone made in the pancreas in response to a meal, which helps the body remove sugar from the blood and store it in fat and muscle for later use

insulin resistance—the tendency for some people, particularly obese people, to respond less well than others to insulin, and therefore to make more insulin than normal to keep blood sugar levels normal

leptin—a hormone made by fat cells that helps regulate body weight and is necessary for puberty to progress

Lupron—the brand name for the main drug used in the United States to treat true precocious puberty, a modified version of GnRH

luteinizing hormone (LH)—the pituitary hormone that stimulates the ovaries or the testes to increase their production of sex hormones; its blood levels are useful in deciding if puberty has started

magnetic resonance imaging (MRI)—a special type of study that allows the physician to look at cross-sectional views to detect abnormal structures or enlarged normal structures inside the body (in the case of early puberty, particularly the area inside the skull near the pituitary gland)

McCune-Albright syndrome—a rare form of precocious puberty characterized by ovarian overactivity, distinctive pigmented skin lesions, and cystlike bone changes

menarche—the time of a girl's first menstrual period

Pediatric Research in Office Settings (PROS)—a network of physicians in private practice, organized by the American Academy of Pediatrics, that conducts various studies, including the study organized by Dr. Herman-Giddens on the age at which healthy girls develop signs of puberty

peripheral precocious puberty—a condition in which the physical changes of puberty with elevated sex hormone levels start at an early age, but there is no activation of the HPG axis, meaning that the problem is in the gonads or the adrenal gland

pituitary—the small gland at the base of the brain that controls the activity of most of the hormone-producing glands in the body, including the ovaries and testes

predicted height—the estimate of adult height a specialist makes based on the child's current height and bone age

premature adrenarche—pubic and/or underarm hair starting at an early age, due to an early increase in production of adrenal androgens

premature thelarche—breast development starting at an early age (usually under age 3) that does not progress or progresses very slowly over time

Tanner stages—the common method of describing how advanced a child is in puberty, based on the scale originally developed by Dr. James Tanner, with separate scales for breast and pubic hair development. Stage 1 means prepubertal (i.e., no breasts or pubic hair) and stage 5 means adultlike in appearance; most children seen for early puberty have stage 2 breasts or pubic hair

target height—the average of the heights of a child's parents, plus 2½ inches for boys and minus 2½ inches for girls; provides an estimate of how tall a child is likely to become as an adult, factoring in genetic potential

thelarche—the time at which breast tissue first appears

true (central) precocious puberty—the physical and hormonal changes of puberty starting at an unusually early age (less than 7 or 8 years depending on the definition one uses) and resulting from early activation of the HPG axis

ultrasound—a type of study that allows physicians to view structures inside the body by bouncing sound waves off them; the pictures are not as sharp as those obtained with an MRI, but it is more often used to make an image of the ovaries and uterus, because it involves no radiation exposure

REFERENCES

Introduction

1. Herman-Giddens, M.E., E.J. Slora, R.C. Wasserman, et al. 1997. Secondary sexual characteristics and menses in young girls seen in office practice: A study from the Pediatrics Research in Office Settings network. *Pediatrics* 99:505–512.
2. Kaplowitz, P.B., S.E. Oberfield, and the Drug and Therapeutics and Executive Committees of the Lawson Wilkins Pediatric Endocrine Society. 1999. Reexamination of the age limit for defining when puberty is precocious in girls in the United States: Implications for evaluation and treatment. *Pediatrics* 104:936–941.
3. Boodman, S. 1999. New guidelines say early puberty may be normal. *The Washington Post,* October 26.
4. McCullough, M. 1999. Early maturing in girls is common, experts say. *The Philadelphia Inquirer,* November 1.
5. Brody, J. 1999. Personal Health: Yesterday's precocious puberty is norm today. *The New York Times,* November 30.
6. Parker-Pope, T. 2000. Rise in early puberty causes parents to ask, "When is it too soon?" *The Wall Street Journal,* July 21.

7. Lemonick, M. 2000. Teens before their time. *Time,* October 30, 66.
8. Belkin, L. 2000. The making of an 8-year-old woman. *The New York Times Magazine,* December 24, 38.
9. Rosenfield, R.L., L.K. Bachrach, S.D. Chernausek, et al. 2000. Current age of onset of puberty. *Pediatrics* 105:115–116.
10. Kolata, G. 2001. Doubters fault theory finding earlier puberty. *The New York Times,* February 20.
11. Kolata, G. 2001. Two endocrinology groups raise doubt on earlier onset of girls' puberty. *The New York Times,* March 3.

Chapter 1

1. Garn, S.M., M. LaVelle, and J.J. Pilkington. 1983. Comparison of fatness in premenarcheal and postmenarcheal girls of the same age. *J. Pediatr.* 103:328–331.
2. Lin-Su, K., M.G. Vogiatsi, and M.I. New. 2002. Body mass index and age at menarche in an adolescent clinic population. *Clin. Pediatr.* 41:501–507.
3. Warren, M.P. 1983. The effects of undernutrition on reproductive function in the human. *Endocr. Rev.* 4:363–377.
4. Marshall, W.A., and J.M. Tanner. 1969. Variations in the pattern of pubertal changes in girls. *Arch. Dis. Child.* 44:291–303.
5. Marti-Henneberg, C., and B. Vizmanos. 1997. The duration of puberty in girls is related to the timing of its onset. *J. Pediatr.* 131:618–621.

Chapter 2

1. Ibanez, L., R. Virdis, N. Potau, et al. 1992. Natural history of premature pubarche: An auxological study. *J. Clin. Endocr. Metab.* 74:254–257.
2. Diamond, F.B., D.I. Shulman, and A.W. Root. 1989. Scrotal hair in infancy. *J. Pediatr.* 114:999–1001.
3. Adams, D.M., P.C. Young, and K.C. Copeland. 1992. Pubic hair in infancy. *Amer. J. Dis. Child.* 146:149–151.
4. Ibanez, L., N. Potau, R. Virdis, et al. 1993. Postpubertal outcome in girls diagnosed of premature adrenarche in childhood: Increased frequency of functional ovarian hyperandrogenism. *J. Clin. Endocr. Metab.* 76:1599–1603.
5. Pescovitz, O.H., K.D. Hench, K.M. Barnes, et al. 1988. Premature thelarche and central precocious puberty: The relationship between clinical presentation and the gonadotropin response to luteinizing hormone-releasing hormone. *J. Clin. Endocr. Metab.* 67:474–479.
6. Salardi, S., E. Cacciari, B. Mainetti, et al. 1998. Outcome of premature thelarche: Relation to puberty and final height. *Arch. Dis. Child.* 79:173–4.
7. Palmert, M.R., H.V. Malin, P.A. Boepple. 1999. Unsustained or slowly progressive puberty in young girls: Initial presentation and long-term follow-up of 20 untreated patients. *J. Clin. Endocr. Metab.* 84:415–423.
8. Fontoura, M., R. Brauner, C. Prevot, and R. Rappoport. 1989. Precocious puberty in girls: Early diagnosis of a slowly progressing variant. *Arch. Dis. Child.* 64:1170–1176.
9. Murram, D., J. Dewhurst, and D.B. Grant. 1983. Premature menarche: A follow-up study. *Arch. Dis. Child.* 58:142–143.

10. Blanco-Garcia, M., D. Evain-Brion, D. Roger, and M. Job. 1985. Isolated menses in prepubertal girls. *Pediatrics* 76:43–47.

Chapter 3

1. Money, J., and J. Neill. 1967. Precocious puberty, IQ, and school acceleration. *Clin. Pediatr.* 6:277–280.
2. Galatzer, A., M.A. Beth-Halachmi, R. Kauli, and Z. Laron. 1984. Intellectual function of girls with precocious puberty. *Pediatrics* 74:246–249.
3. Ehrhardt, A.A., and H.F.L. Meyer-Bahlburg. 1994. Psychosocial aspects of precocious puberty. *Hormone Res.* 41(suppl 2):30–35.
4. Sonis, W.A., F. Comite, J. Blue, O.H. Pescovitz, C.W. Rahn, K.D. Hench, et al. 1985. Behavior problems and social competence in girls with true precocious puberty. *J. Pediatr.* 106:156–160.
5. Xhrouet-Heinrich, D., K. Lagrou, C. Heinrich, et al. 1997. Longitudinal study of behavioral and affective patterns in girls with central precocious puberty during long-acting triptorelin therapy. *Acta. Paediatr.* 86:808–815.
6. Ehrhardt, A.A., H.F.L. Meyer-Bahlberg, and J.J. Bell. 1984. Idiopathic precocious puberty in girls: Psychiatric follow-up in adolescence. *J. Am. Acad. Child Psych.* 23:23–33.
7. Baumann, D.A., M.A. Landolt, R. Wetterwald, et al. 2001. Psychological evaluation of young women after medical treatment for central precocious puberty. *Horm. Res.* 56:45–50.
8. Gruelich, W.W., and S.I. Pyle. *Radiographic Atlas of*

Skeletal Development of the Hand and Wrist. Stanford University Press, 1959.

9. Bayley, N., and S.R. Pinneau. 1952. Tables for predicting adult height from skeletal age: Revised for use with Greulich-Pyle hand standards. *J. Pediatr.* 50:432–441.

10. Loder, R.T., D.T. Estle, K. Morrison, et al. 1993. Applicability of the Greulich and Pyle skeletal age standards to black and white children of today. *Am. J. Dis. Child.* 147:1329–1333.

11. Bar, A., B. Linder, E.H. Sobel, P. Saenger, and J. Martino-Nardi. 1995. Bayley-Pinneau method of height prediction in girls with central precocious puberty: Correlation with adult height. *J. Pediatr.* 126:955–958.

12. Zachmann, M., B. Sobradillo, M. Frank, et al. 1978. Bayley-Pinneau, Roche-Wainer-Thissen, and Tanner height predictions in normal children and in patients with various pathological conditions. *J. Pediatr.* 93:749–755.

13. Shangold, M.M., M. Kelly, A.S. Berkeley, K.S. Freedman, and S. Groshen. 1989. Relationship between menarcheal age and adult height. *South Medical J.* 82:443–445.

Chapter 4

1. Tanner, M., and P.B. Eveleth. 1975. Variability between populations in growth and development at puberty. In Berebberg, S.R., ed. *Puberty, Biologic and Psychosocial Components.* Leiden: H.E. Stenfert Kroese, 256–273.

2. Frisch, R.E., and J.W. McArthur. 1974. Menstrual cycles: Fatness as a determinant of minimum weight for

height necessary for their maintenance and onset. *Science* 185:949–951.

3. Reynolds, E.L., and J.V. Wines. 1948. Individual difference in physical changes associated with adolescence in girls. *Am. J. Dis. Child.* 75:329–350.

4. Nicolson, A.B., and C. Hanley. 1953. Indices of physiological maturity: Derivation and interrelationships. *Child Dev.* 24:3–38.

5. Harlan, W.R., E.A. Harlan, and C.P. Grillo. 1980. Secondary sex characteristics of girls 12–17 years of age: The U.S. Health Examination Survey. *J. Pediatr.* 96:1074–1078.

6. Roche, A.F., R. Wellens, K.M. Attie, and R.M. Siervogel. 1995. The timing of sexual maturation in a group of U.S. white youths. *J. Pediatr. Endocr. Metab.* 8:11–18.

7. Marshall, W.A., and J.M. Tanner. 1969. Variations in the pattern of pubertal changes in girls. *Arch. Dis. Child.* 44:291–303.

8. Herman-Giddens, M.E., A.D. Sandler, and N.E. Friedman. 1998. Sexual precocity in girls: An association with sexual abuse? *Am. J. Dis. Child.* 142:431–433.

9. Herman-Giddens, M.E., E.J. Slora, R.C. Wasserman, et al. 1997. Secondary sexual characteristics and menses in young girls seen in office practice: A study from the Pediatrics Research in Office Settings network. *Pediatrics* 99:505–512.

10. Wu, T., P. Mendola, and G.M. Buck. 2002. Ethnic differences in the presence of secondary sex characteristics and menarche among U.S. girls: The third National Health and Nutrition Examination Survey, 1988–1994. *Pediatrics* 110:752–757.

11. Anderson, S.E., G.E. Dallal, and A. Must. 2003. Relative weight and race influence average age at menarche: Results from two nationally representative surveys of U.S. girls 25 years apart. *Pediatrics* 111:844–850.

12. Freedman, D.S., L.K. Khan, M.K. Serdula, et al. 2000. Secular trends in height among children during 2 decades: The Bogalusa Heart Study. *Arch. Pediatr. Adolesc. Med.* 154:155–161.

13. Freedman, D.S., L.K. Khan, M.K. Serdula, et al. 2002. Relation of menarche to race, time period, and anthropomorphic dimensions: The Bogalusa Heart Study. *Pediatrics* 110:e43.

Chapter 5

1. Fara, G.M., G. Del Corvo, S. Bernuzzi, et al. 1979. Epidemic of breast enlargement in an Italian school. *Lancet* II:295–297.

2. Saenz de Rodriguez, C.A., A.M. Bongiovanni, and L. Conde de Borrego. 1985. An epidemic of precocious pubertal development in Puerto Rican children. *J. Pediatr.* 107:393–396.

3. Paretsch, C-J., and W.G. Sippell. 2001. Pathogenesis and epidemiology of precocious puberty: Effects of exogenous oestrogens. *Human Reproduction Update* 7:292–302.

4. Zimmerman, P.A., G.L. Francis, and M. Poth. 1995. Hormone-containing cosmetics may cause signs of early sexual development. *Mil. Med.* 160:628–630.

5. Gladen, B.C., B. Ragan, and W.J. Rogan. 2000. Pubertal growth and development and prenatal and

lactational exposure to polychlorinated biphenyls and dichlorophenyl dichloroethene. *J. Pediatr.* 136:490–496.

6. Blanck, H.M., M. Marcus, P.E. Tolbert, et al. 2000. Age at menarche and Tanner stage in girls exposed *in utero* and postnatally to polybrominated biphenyl. *Epidemiology* 11:641–647.

7. Krstevska-Komstantinova, M., C. Charlier, M. Craen, et al. 2001. Sexual precocity after immigration from developing countries to Belgium: Evidence of previous exposure to organochlorine pesticides. *Human Reproduction Update* 16:1020–1026.

8. Colon, I., D. Caro, C.J. Bourdony, and O. Rosario. 2000. Identification of phthalate esters in the serum of young Puerto Rican girls with premature breast development. *Environ. Health Perspect.* 108:895–900.

9. Belsky, J., et al. 1991. Childhood experience, interpersonal development and reproductive strategy: An evolutionary theory of socialization. *Child Dev.* 62(4):647–670.

10. Ellis, B.J., and J. Garber. 2000. Psychosocial antecedents of variation in girls' pubertal timing: Maternal depression, stepfather presence, and marital and family stress. *Child Dev.* 71:485–501.

11. Hulanicka, B., L. Gronkiewicz, and J. Koniarek. 2001. Effect of familial distress on growth and maturation of girls: A longitudinal study. *Am. J. Human Biol.* 13:771–776.

12. National Center for Health Statistics, U.S. Dept. of Health and Human Services (cited in the *World Almanac and Book of Facts 2002*, World Almanac Books, 877).

13. Troiano, R.P., K.M. Flegal, R.J. Kuczmarski, S.M. Campbell, and C.L. Johnson. 1995. Overweight

prevalence and trends for children and adolescents: The National Health and Nutrition Examination Surveys, 1963 to 1991. *Arch. Pediatr. Adolesc. Med.* 149:1085–1091.

14. Ogden, C.L., K.M. Flegal, M.D. Carroll, and C.L. Johnson. 2002. Prevalence and trends in overweight among US children and adolescents, 1999–2000. *JAMA* 288:1728–1732.

15. Daniels, S.R., P.R. Khoury, and J.A. Morrison. 1997. The utility of body mass index as a measure of body fatness in children and adolescents: Differences by race and gender. *Pediatrics* 99:804–807.

16. Rosner, B., R. Prineas, J. Loggie, and S.R. Daniels. 1998. Percentiles for body mass index in U.S. children 5 to 17 years of age. *J. Pediatr.* 132:211–222.

17. Kaplowitz, P.B., E.J. Slora, R.C. Wasserman, S.E. Pedlow, and M.E. Herman-Giddens. 2001. Earlier onset of puberty in girls: Relation to increased body mass index and race. *Pediatrics* 108:347–353.

18. He, Q., and J. Karlberg. 2001. BMI gain in childhood and its association with height gain, timing of puberty, and final height. *Pediatr. Res.* 49:244–251.

19. Davison, K.K., E.J. Susman, and L.L. Birch. 2003. Percent of body fat at age 5 predicts earlier pubertal development among girls at age 9. *Pediatrics* 111:815–821.

20. Barash, I.A., C.C. Cheung, D.S. Weigle, et al. 1996. Leptin is a metabolic signal to the reproductive system. *Endocrinology* 137:3144–3147.

21. Blum, W.F., P. Englaro, S. Hanitsch, et al. 1997. Plasma leptin levels in healthy children and adolescents: Dependence on body mass index, body fat mass,

gender, pubertal stage, and testosterone. *J. Clin. Endocrinol. Metab.* 82:2904–2910.

22. Garcia-Mayor, R.V., A. Andrade, M. Rios, et al. 1997. Serum leptin levels in normal children: Relationship to age, gender, body mass index, pituitary-gonadal hormones, and pubertal stage. *J. Clin. Endocrinol. Metab.* 82:2849–2855.

23. Ahmed, M.L., K.K.L. Ong, D.J. Morrell, et al. 1999. Longitudinal study of leptin concentrations during puberty: Sex differences and relationship to changes in body composition. *J. Clin. Endocrinol. Metab.* 84:899–905.

24. Herman-Giddens, M.E., L. Wang, and G. Koch. 2001. Secondary sexual characteristics in boys: Estimates from the National Health and Nutrition Examination Survey III, 1988–1994. *Arch. Pediatr. Adolesc. Med.* 155:1022–1028.

25. Vignolo, M., A. Naselli, E. Di Battista, et al. 1988. Growth and development in simple obesity. *Eur. J. Pediatr.* 147:242–244.

26. Wang, Y. 2002. Is obesity associated with earlier sexual maturation? A comparison of the association in American boys vs. girls. *Pediatrics* 110:903–910.

27. Morrison, J.A., B. Barton, F. Biro, et al. 1994. Sexual maturation and obesity in 9- and 10-year-old black and white girls: The National Heart, Lung, and Blood Institute Growth and Health Study. *J. Pediatr.* 124:889–895.

28. Arslanian, S., C. Suprasongsin, and J. Janosky. 1997. Insulin secretion and sensitivity in black vs. white prepubertal healthy children. *J. Clin. Endocrinol. Metab.* 82:1923–1927.

29. Wong, W.W., M. Nicolson, J.E. Stuff, et al. 1998.
    Serum leptin concentrations in Caucasian and
    African-American girls. *J. Clin. Endocrinol. Metab.*
    83:3574–3577.

Chapter 7

1. Chalumeau, M., W. Chemaitilly, C. Trivin, et al. 2002.
   Central precocious puberty in girls: An evidence-based
   diagnosis tree to predict central nervous system
   abnormalities. *Pediatrics* 109:61–67.
2. Kaplowitz, P.B. 2002. Precocious puberty in girls and
   the risk of a central nervous system abnormality: The
   elusive search for diagnostic certainty. *Pediatrics*
   109:139–141.

Chapter 8

1. Boepple, P.A., J. Mansfield, M.E. Wierman, et al. 1986.
   Use of a long acting agonist of gonadotropin-releasing
   hormone in the treatment of precocious puberty.
   Endocrine Rev. 7:24–33.
2. Belchetz, P.E., T.M. Plant, Y. Nakai, E.J. Keogh,
   and E. Knobil. 1978. Hypophyseal responses to
   continuous and intermittent delivery of hypothalamic
   gonadotropin-releasing hormone. *Science* 202:631–634.
3. Comite, F., G.B. Cutler, J. Rivier, et al. 1981.
   Short-term treatment of idiopathic precocious puberty
   with a long-acting analogue of luteinizing
   hormone-releasing hormone. *N. Engl. J. Med.*
   305:1546–1550.

4. Comite, F., F. Cassorla, K.M. Barnes, et al. 1986. Luteinizing hormone releasing hormone analogue therapy for central precocious puberty: Long-term effect on somatic growth, bone maturation, and predicted height. *JAMA* 255:2613–2616.

5. Lin, T-H, M.E. LePage, M. Henzi, and J.L. Kirkland. 1986. Intranasal nafarelin: An LH-RH analogue treatment of gonadotropin-dependent precocious puberty. *J. Pediatr.* 109:954–958.

6. Kappy, M., T. Stuart, A. Perelman, and R. Clemons. 1989. Suppression of gonadotropin secretion by a long-acting gonadotropin-releasing hormone analog (leuprolide acetate, Lupron Depot) in children with precocious puberty. *J. Clin. Endocrinol. Metab.* 69:1087–1089.

7. Neely, E.K., R.L. Hintz, B. Parker, et al. 1992. Two-year results of treatment with depot leuprolide acetate for central precocious puberty. *J. Pediatr.* 121:634–640.

8. Kletter, G.B., and R.P. Kelch. 1994. Effects of gonadotropin-releasing hormone analog therapy on adult short stature in precocious puberty. *J. Clin. Endocrinol. Metab.* 79:331–334.

9. Paul, D., F.A. Conte, M.M. Grumbach, and S.L. Kaplan. 1995. Long-term effect of gonadotropin-releasing hormone agonist therapy in final and near final height in 26 children with true precocious puberty treated at a median age of less than 5 years. *J. Clin. Endocrinol. Metab.* 80:546–551.

10. Rosenfield, R.L. 1994. Selection of children with precocious puberty for treatment with gonadotropin-releasing hormone analogs. *J. Pediatr.* 124:989–991.

11. Lazar, L., R. Kauli, A. Pertzelan, and M. Phillip. 2002.

Gonadotropin-suppressive therapy in girls with early and fast puberty affects the pace of puberty but not total pubertal growth or final height. *J. Clin. Endocrinol. Metab.* 87:2090–2094.

12. Kreiter, M., S. Burstein, R.L. Rosenfield, et al. 1990. Preserving height potential in girls with idiopathic true precocious puberty. *J. Pediatr.* 117:364–370.

13. Palmert, M.R., H.V. Malin, and P.A. Boepple. 1999. Unsustained or slowly progressive puberty in young girls: Initial presentation and long-term follow-up of 20 untreated patients. *J. Clin. Endocrinol. Metab.* 84:415–423.

14. Leger, J., R. Reynaud, and P. Czernichow. 2000. Do all girls with apparent idiopathic precocious puberty require gonadotropin-releasing hormone agonist treatment? *J. Pediatr.* 137:819–825.

15. Klein, K.O. 1999. Editorial: Precocious puberty: Who has it? Who should be treated? *J. Clin. Endocrinol. Metab.* 84:411–413.

16. Carel, J-C, N. Lahlou, O. Jaramillo, et al. 2002. Treatment of central precocious puberty by subcutaneous injections of Leuprorelin 3-month depot (11.25 mg). *J. Clin. Endocrinol. Metab.* 87:4111–4116.

17. Lee, P.A. 1994. Laboratory monitoring of children with precocious puberty. *Arch. Pediatr. Adolesc. Med.* 148:369–376.

18. Bhatia, S., K. Neely, and D.M. Wilson. 2002. Serum luteinizing hormone rises within minutes after depot leuprolide injection: Implications for monitoring therapy. *Pediatrics* 109:e30.

ABOUT THE AUTHOR

Dr. Paul Kaplowitz grew up in the Bronx, New York. He attended the University of Michigan, and obtained both an M.D. and a PhD from the University of Chicago. He did his pediatric and pediatric endocrine training at the University of North Carolina in Chapel Hill. For twenty-one years he was on the faculty of the Department of Pediatrics at the Virginia Commonwealth University School of Medicine in Richmond, Virginia. He is presently the Chief of Endocrinology at the Children's National Medical Center in Washington, D.C. He is the author of more than forty articles, many dealing with growth and puberty, and has been listed in *The Best Doctors in America* since 1998. He has appeared on *Today* twice to discuss early puberty in girls, and has been quoted in numerous publications on the subject. He is married to Dr. Lisa Kaplowitz and has two sons, Joshua and Daniel, and a grandson, Elijah.